AF241376

TRUE CRIME FILES

24 CHILLING TRUE CRIME STORIES YOU'VE NEVER HEARD OF

SCOTT MATTHEWS

Copyright © 2026 Scott Matthews

All rights reserved. No part of this publication may be reproduced, distributed or transmitted in any form or by any means, including photocopying, recording, or other electronic or mechanical methods, without the prior written permission of the publisher, except in the case of brief quotations embodied in critical reviews and certain other non-commercial uses permitted by copyright law.

Trademarked names appear throughout this book. Rather than use a trademark symbol with every occurrence of a trademarked name, names are used in an editorial fashion, with no intention of infringement of the respective owner's trademark. The information in this book is distributed on an "as is" basis, without warranty. Although every precaution has been taken in the preparation of this work, neither the author nor the publisher shall have any liability to any person or entity with respect to any loss or damage caused or alleged to be caused directly or indirectly by the information contained in this book.

Monsters are real, and ghosts are real too. They live inside us, and sometimes, they win.

– Stephen King

CONTENTS

INTRODUCTION

Welcome to the shadows.

Most people believe they understand the limits of human depravity. They recognize the names of "household" monsters and the cases that dominate mainstream media. But the true nature of evil doesn't always make the front page; it often lingers in the quiet corners of the world, hidden in cold files that have gathered dust or in stories that were too strange, too local, or too terrifying to be widely told.

True Crime Files: 24 Chilling True Crime Stories You've Never Heard Of peels back the curtain on cases that defy easy explanation. This is an expedition into the darkest corridors of the human psyche, spanning the globe from the desolate "Valley of Death" in Norway to the cryptic, taunting letters of Circleville. These accounts prove that truth is not only stranger than fiction — it is far more ruthless.

Within these pages, you will encounter a diverse gallery of darkness. I explore the manipulative power of belief in chapters like "The Yerba Buena Cult" and the chilling conviction of "Jesus was an Alien." The book dives into high-stakes deception, from the audacity of the "Carnegie Heiress" to the historical fraud of the "Hitler Diaries." For those fascinated by the hunt, I track predators like the "National Forest Killer" and the elusive, faceless entities behind Japan's "Monster with 21 Faces." These are but a few of the twenty-four harrowing accounts waiting for you in these pages.

But the horror doesn't stop with the infamous. Beyond these names lies a deeper, more personal brand of terror — a reminder that the "sleepwalker" in the room down the hall, or the silent van parked in a driveway nearby, might be hiding a secret that would freeze your blood.

Turn the page, lock your doors, and prepare yourself. The world is a much darker place than you imagined.

1

THE SLEEPWALKER

In the world of aspiring online creators, Robert Eugene Crimo III was, for a brief time, a quiet success story. He was a sad, neglected, and lonely kid from an affluent Chicago suburb who found an outlet, and even a small following, through a rap career he built from scratch on YouTube and Spotify. But as his personal life began to unravel under the weight of family dysfunction, financial ruin, and profound depression, the music that was once his salvation began to mirror a much darker internal reality. The mellow, sad-sounding tracks gave way to cryptic videos filled with violent imagery and nihilistic pronouncements. This descent culminated on July 4, 2022, when the rapper known as "Awake" climbed to a rooftop overlooking his hometown's Independence Day parade and rained down a hail of bullets on the unsuspecting crowd below, leaving a trail of casualties, unanswered questions, and bizarre conspiracy theories in his wake.

Robert, who went by Awake later in his rap career, was born on September 20, 2000, and was raised for his entire life in the Lake County area of Illinois, primarily in the city of Highland Park. On the surface, it was an idyllic place to grow up. A wealthy suburb of Chicago, it was known as the picturesque filming location for movies like *Ferris Bueller's Day Off* and as the onetime home of basketball legend Michael Jordan.

Awake's family was middle-class; his father, Robert Crimo Jr., was a local businessman, and his mother, Denise, listed her occupation as a homeopathic healer. But unlike many of their neighbors in the affluent community, the Crimo family was deeply dysfunctional, and the signs of neglect began when Awake was just a toddler.

When he was two years old, his mother drove him to a local Toys "R" Us on a hot day and left him alone in the car with the windows rolled up for nearly half an hour. A concerned passerby saw the child and contacted the police. Denise was arrested and charged with child endangerment, to which she pleaded guilty. This incident was a grim foreshadowing of the chaotic and neglectful environment that would define Awake's childhood. While his father was not actively abusive, he was largely absent, consumed by his work. In 2008, after running a few other stores, Robert Jr. opened a popular deli and pantry in town, a "mom and pop" operation that became a local hangout spot. On its opening day, photos captured a seemingly happy family, and young Awake was often seen running around the store while his father worked.

But this picture of familial harmony was a facade. The dysfunction that plagued the Crimo marriage was not kept behind closed doors; it was on full public display. Robert and Denise would frequently engage in heated, screaming arguments right in the middle of the deli, in front of friends, customers, and their own children. One of Robert's friends later recalled the intense discomfort these public fights caused, remarking, "If that's the public arguments, I can only imagine the private ones." Soon, the verbal altercations escalated into physical violence. Between 2009 and 2013, police were called to the family home nearly twenty times, with nine of those calls related to domestic violence, usually involving Denise throwing objects at or hitting Robert. The most serious incident occurred in 2010, when Robert called the police to report that his wife had attacked him with a screwdriver. But once at the station, he recanted his story, refusing to press charges — a common pattern in their volatile relationship.

The parents' neglect was also apparent at school. A former coach recalled that Awake and his younger brother were often left behind by their "flighty" mother, who would simply forget to pick them up after their after-school programs had ended, leaving them stranded for hours while their father was busy at the deli. It was in the midst of this turmoil that Awake, at the age of eleven, sought refuge in music. He decided he wanted to become a rapper, creating online accounts on various platforms and adopting the stage name "Awake the Rapper."

During his middle school years, Awake was described by classmates as a weird, soft-spoken kid who showed little interest in school or his peers. He started to open up a bit after discovering skateboarding, a hobby that allowed him to make a few friends. He also created a YouTube channel, where his earliest videos were mostly do-it-yourself (DIY) tutorials on how to maintain a skateboard. But by the time he entered high school, this brief period of social connection had faded. He reverted to being a loner, a distant figure who was always by himself. He continued to release music throughout his high school years, but his disinterest in academics was profound. Just before his junior year, he dropped out, a decision his father explained to a neighbor was due to his son's "emotional issues."

Now free from the structure of school, Awake dedicated himself completely to his rapper persona. He began to cover his hands, arms, and even his face in tattoos, including the word "AWAKE" inked in block letters just above his right eyebrow. He drove a car emblazoned with anime stickers and the words "Pussy Mobile" written across the back, and he was known to ride an electric bike around the neighborhood while blasting heavy metal music. In 2016, at sixteen, he had his first minor run-in with the law for possession of tobacco. That same year, he had his first taste of viral success with a song called "By the Pond," which he released with another artist named Atlas. The music video for the song eventually garnered around three million views across all platforms before Awake, for reasons unknown, deleted it entirely, an act that only added to his growing online mystique. He released his first full album, *Messages*, in 2017, followed by two more in 2018. He developed a small but consistent following, with his tracks reliably pulling in several thousand views each. His early music was often described as mellow, slow, and sad-sounding rap.

But as Awake's music career was beginning to take off, his family's life was imploding. In 2019, Robert Crimo Jr., facing dwindling business at his deli and mounting debts, launched a bizarre and ill-fated campaign for mayor of Highland Park. He ran against Nancy Roering, who, in a strange twist of fate, had been Awake's Cub Scout leader years earlier. Robert Jr.'s campaign was a non-starter; he was never seen campaigning and received no donations other than one he gave to himself. He was defeated in a landslide. Shortly after, the deli was forced to close, and the family was plunged into financial ruin, with one lender suing Robert for over $750,000. For Awake, who was living in a small apartment on the back of his father's property, the future was looking increasingly bleak.

It was during this period of intense family stress that Awake's own mental health took a nosedive. He had become deeply depressed, and in April 2019, he attempted suicide. Just a few months later, in September, a family member called the police after Awake, brandishing a collection of knives, threatened to "kill everyone." When police arrived, his parents downplayed the incident, and while he wasn't charged with a crime, officers did confiscate sixteen knives, a dagger, and a sword from the home. Crucially, the police also filed a "clear and present danger" report, a legal designation intended to prevent individuals who pose a threat to themselves or others from obtaining a firearm license.

Awake's online persona and real-world behavior began to take a strange turn. He started showing up at Donald Trump rallies, sometimes dressed in a "Where's Waldo?" costume, a goofy act that led many to believe he was simply trolling. At the same time, his music videos grew darker and more cryptic. One video, for a song called "Toy Soldier," featured crude animations of a school shooter, police, and injured victims. Another, for a re-release of his song "On My Mind," depicted Awake in a classroom, first sitting at a teacher's desk, and then suddenly clad in makeshift tactical gear, including a bicycle helmet, as the room is shown littered with what appear to be bullet casings. The video was filled with obscure references to the video game *Call of Duty: Zombies*, a game he was known to be a fan of. Without his own commentary, it was impossible to know if these were artistic expressions, bizarre tributes, or the fantasies of a deeply disturbed young man.

His personal life continued its downward spiral. His parents had separated, and the mortgage company had begun foreclosure proceedings on the family home. He was shot down by a female coworker at Panera

Bread whom he had become infatuated with, a rejection that some have speculated was a major contributing factor to his deteriorating mindset. It was in this state of hopelessness and despair that Awake made a fateful decision. He applied for a Firearm Owner's Identification (FOID) card. Because he was not yet twenty-one, he needed a sponsor, and his father, Robert Crimo Jr., agreed to be that sponsor. In a catastrophic failure of the system, the Illinois State Police, for reasons that remain unclear, chose not to act on the "clear and present danger" report they had on file. Within a few months, Awake, having passed a background check, had his license. He immediately began purchasing weapons. Between June and September of 2020, he legally bought five guns, including a Smith & Wesson M&P-15 semi-automatic rifle.

As he was amassing an arsenal, his online activities grew more sinister. Under the username "Awake47," he became a frequent lurker on a gore website called Documenting Reality, a private forum where users share graphic videos and images of real-life violence and death. He began to regularly comment on footage related to mass shootings. By this point, his descent seemed complete.

In February 2021, he self-published a twenty-eight-page book called *Arcturus*, which he described as a manifesto. It was composed entirely of an undeciphered sequence of numbers and remains an unsolved mystery. He was done with music. In his final, chilling video, uploaded just before the attack, he narrated his thoughts over a montage of his previous work. "I need to just do it," he said in a monotone voice. "It is my destiny. Everything has led up to this. Nothing can stop me, not even myself... Like a sleepwalker, walking blindly into the night."

On the morning of July 4, 2022, as the town of Highland Park prepared for its first Independence Day parade in two years, Awake put his plan into action. He prepared his Smith & Wesson rifle and stashed another gun in his mother's car. To conceal his highly recognizable face tattoos and to blend in with the panicked crowd after the attack, he disguised himself in women's clothing. He made his way to the Ross Cosmetics building on Central Avenue, climbed an unsecured staircase to the roof, and set up what he felt was the perfect sniper's nest. At 10:14 a.m., just as the parade began to pass below, he took aim and opened fire. In the span of just a few minutes, he fired eighty-three rounds into the crowd, reloading his rifle twice. The scene below erupted into mass chaos. People screamed, cried, and ran in all directions, scrambling for cover. In total, forty-five people were struck by his gunfire.

His escape plan worked flawlessly. As law enforcement swarmed the scene, Awake, still in his disguise, simply blended in with the terrified paradegoers and walked away, dropping his rifle in the street as he fled. He went home, borrowed his mother's car, and went on the run. The scene he left behind was one of utter devastation. Forty-eight people were injured, one of whom was left permanently paralyzed. Seven people were killed: Katherine Goldstein, Irina McCarthy, Kevin McCarthy, Stephen Strauss, Jacki Sundheim, Nicolas Toledo-Zaragoza, and Eduardo Uvaldo. The parents of a two-year-old boy, Irina and Kevin McCarthy, had both been killed, leaving their son an orphan.

Awake drove north toward Madison, Wisconsin, where he considered carrying out a similar attack on another parade but ultimately decided against it. The manhunt, meanwhile, was in full force. Police quickly found the abandoned rifle and, using security camera footage, identified Awake and the car he was driving. Eight hours after the attack, following a tip from a citizen who recognized the vehicle, police surrounded him and he was arrested without incident. In his confession, he admitted to aiming at people from the waist up, shooting to kill. He referred to the panicked crowd as "sleepwalkers and zombies," a chilling echo of his final video.

The legal fallout was swift. Awake was indicted on 117 felonies, including twenty-one counts of first-degree murder — three for each of the seven victims he killed. His father, Robert Crimo Jr., was also arrested and charged with seven counts of reckless conduct for sponsoring his son's gun license, to which he eventually pleaded guilty and served a brief jail sentence. After a series of bizarre legal maneuvers, including an initial "not guilty" plea and a flirtation with conspiracy theories claiming he was a "patsy" in a false flag operation, Awake finally pleaded guilty to all remaining counts just hours before his trial was set to begin. He was sentenced to seven consecutive life sentences without the possibility of parole.

To this day, we still don't know exactly why he did it. He left no manifesto that could be understood, and in his confession, he offered no clear motive. It was likely a confluence of factors: a lifetime of neglect, profound mental health struggles, personal and financial failures, and a desperate, nihilistic desire to lash out at the world and achieve a dark form of infamy. He is now housed in an undisclosed federal prison, his location kept secret for security reasons. The rapper who called himself Awake has finally been silenced, but the echoes of his final, violent act will haunt the community of Highland Park forever.

2

A CHILDHOOD SENTENCED

It was the last day of school in Lake Worth, Florida, May 26, 2000. An electric buzz of impending freedom filled the hallways of Lake Worth Middle School. Lockers slammed shut for the final time, the sound echoing like a punctuation mark at the end of a long year. Students, their minds already on summer vacation, chattered with an excitement that was almost tangible. In just a few hours, the final bell would ring, releasing them into three months of sun-drenched, unstructured bliss. But inside a classroom, a single moment of a teenage impulse, born from a volatile mix of anger, immaturity, and access to a deadly weapon, was about to rewrite the lives of everyone present. A day that should have been defined by celebration would instead become a nightmare, and a quiet middle school in a Florida suburb would become the epicenter of a fierce national debate about crime, punishment, and the very nature of justice in America.

At the center of this tragedy was thirteen-year-old Nathaniel Brazill. To his teachers, he was no ordinary student. They described him as bright, funny, and at times, even charming. He was an honor student with a perfect attendance record, the kind of kid principals might rely on to help settle minor schoolyard disputes. But beneath that young, likable facade was a simmering anger, a deep well of turmoil fed by a chaotic and abusive home life that no one at the school fully understood. On that fateful last day of school, he had been suspended earlier for a minor infraction — throwing water balloons in the school cafeteria with friends. Upset and fuming, he was sent home before he had the chance to say goodbye to a girl he had a crush on, his first serious girlfriend who had given him his first kiss just six days earlier. In Nathaniel's adolescent mind, this perceived rejection was an unbearable injustice. He rode his bicycle home, but not to begin his summer vacation. He went to retrieve a .25-caliber handgun that belonged to his grandfather, tucked it away, and returned to the school.

He made his way to the classroom of his seventh-grade English teacher, thirty-five-year-old Barry Grunow. Grunow was, by Nathaniel's own account, his favorite teacher, a man he liked and respected. Nathaniel stood at the classroom door and asked to be allowed inside to speak with two female students, including the girl he wanted to see before the summer break began. Grunow, likely seeing a suspended student trying to circumvent the rules, refused his request. The confrontation was brief, a simple exchange between a teacher enforcing discipline and a student pushing back. But Nathaniel was armed. He pulled the small, silver handgun from his pocket. Accounts of what happened next would become the central dispute of his trial. The defense would argue that Mr. Grunow, not taking the threat seriously enough, was met with a cocked gun, an act of intimidation that went horribly wrong. Nathaniel aimed the weapon at his teacher, and in front of a room full of stunned classmates, he fired a single shot. The bullet struck Barry Grunow in the face, killing him instantly. As his favorite teacher lay dying on the classroom floor, Nathaniel ran. The nation was shocked. How could a boy so young, an honor student with no prior history of disciplinary problems, commit such a violent and senseless act? Was this a cold-blooded murder, or a tragic accident born from a child's catastrophic lack of judgment?

The wheels of the justice system turned swiftly. Nathaniel was arrested on the same day as the shooting. The legal framework in Florida at the time, however, was undergoing a dramatic shift. A "tough on crime" mentality had led to changes in laws across the country, blurring the lines between the juvenile and the adult justice systems. There was a time, not so long ago, when a thirteen-year-old who committed even a heinous crime would have been processed through a juvenile system focused on rehabilitation. But by the year 2000, a new philosophy had taken hold: if a child commits an adult crime, they must pay as an adult. In fifteen states, including Florida, the decision of whether to charge a child as an adult was left entirely to the discretion of prosecutors, many of whom were elected officials eager to project a tough image.

Nathaniel Brazill found himself caught in this new legal landscape. The prosecution, brushing aside considerations of his age, mental maturity, and troubled personal situation, decided to try him as an adult for first-degree murder. The case ignited a fierce debate across the country. Should children, whose brains are not yet fully developed and who are legally prohibited from driving, voting, or serving in the military, be locked away in adult prisons for the rest of their lives? Or does a society have a responsibility to seek rehabilitation for its youngest and most troubled offenders? For Nathaniel Brazill, the answer was about to be decided in a courtroom.

The trial became a battle of two starkly contrasting narratives. The prosecution, led by Mark Shiner, painted Nathaniel as a cold-blooded, remorseless killer who was incapable of being rehabilitated. Shiner argued that the killing was premeditated, pointing to statements Nathaniel allegedly made before the shooting that indicated he had planned the act. He repeatedly drew the jury's attention to Nathaniel's stoic and blank demeanor in the courtroom, using it as proof of his lack of remorse. "This defendant's demeanor sends chills up my spine," Shiner told the judge during the sentencing hearing. "Let us not forget a man's life has been taken away," he said after the sentencing, describing the shooting as a "heinous crime committed by a young man with a difficult personality who should be behind bars."

The defense, led by attorney Robert Udell, did not deny that Nathaniel fired the fatal shot. Their entire case hinged on the argument that it was a tragic, unintentional accident. Udell contended that Nathaniel, in a moment of immature fury, only intended to scare his teacher and thought the gun's safety was on when he pointed it at him. They argued that a scared thirteen-year-old boy had been unwittingly thrust into an adult world, and his blank demeanor was not a sign of a sociopath, but rather a coping mechanism for a child accustomed to bottling up his emotions in the face of overwhelming trauma. "He's a child and that's who committed this crime," Udell pleaded with the judge, asking for a sentence of twelve years.

During the emotional sentencing hearing, defense lawyers and psychologists finally revealed the full extent of the turmoil that had been building in Nathaniel's life, painting a picture of a boy drowning in problems that no adult had seemed to notice. His family life was plagued by instability and violence. His mother, Polly Powell, had been in a series of abusive relationships since he was a young boy. Police had been called to their home for domestic incidents on at least seven occasions in the six years leading up to the shooting. Nathaniel had been forced at times to physically intervene in fights between his mother and one of his stepfathers. Another stepfather had refused to let him live in the family home, forcing him to spend nights at his grandmother's house. His biological father was not a constant presence in his life. According to defense experts, Nathaniel learned from a very young age to keep his emotions locked away, to present a stoic exterior no matter what chaos swirled around him.

Just months before the shooting, this fragile stability completely shattered. The month Nathaniel turned thirteen, his mother was diagnosed with breast cancer. His grades, once stellar, began to drop, and in a letter to Mr. Grunow, the very teacher he would later kill, he made references to suicide. He was reportedly fascinated with weapons and dreamed of a career in law enforcement or the military, spending his spare time playing fighter pilot simulation games and visiting military websites. His mother, Polly Powell, took the stand and, between sobs, pleaded for mercy for her son. "I don't know what happened to my baby," she said, adding that if her personal problems and poor choices in men had contributed to his actions, "I take full responsibility."

The highly emotional trial featured the testimony of twenty-three of Nathaniel's classmates, many of whom broke down on the stand as they recalled the horrifying moment when a well-liked, mild-mannered boy shot their beloved teacher. After sixteen hours of deliberation, the jury of nine women and three men returned with a verdict. They rejected the prosecution's argument for first-degree murder, deciding that the shooting was not premeditated. Instead, they found Nathaniel Brazill guilty of second-degree murder with a firearm. While this spared him the mandatory sentence of life without parole, under Florida's sentencing laws, the judge was still required to impose a sentence of twenty-five years to life.

On July 27, 2001, Nathaniel Brazill, now fourteen years old, stood shackled in an orange prison uniform, silent and expressionless, as Judge Richard Wennett pronounced his fate. He was sentenced to twenty-eight years in an adult prison, without the possibility of parole. The sentence would be followed by two years of house arrest and five years of probation. The judge also ordered him to earn his high school equivalency diploma and enroll in an anger management course while in custody. He would be held in a juvenile correction center until he turned eighteen, at which point he would be transferred to an adult prison to serve out the remainder of his sentence.

The reaction to the sentence was deeply divided. The Grunow family, with the exception of the victim's widow, Pam, had asked for the maximum penalty of life in prison and felt the twenty-eight-year term was disappointingly lenient. Barry Grunow's brother, Kurt, told Court TV he was "very disappointed" and felt the jury must have been watching a different trial. Nathaniel's mother, on the other hand, was grateful for what she saw as the judge's leniency. "I was hoping for less," she said, "but I know my son will be home someday."

Nathaniel's life was now defined by prison walls. The months of confinement in an adult county jail while awaiting trial had begun to harden him, forcing him to turn inward in a way that came across as sullen and uncaring. Deputies testified that in his holding cell, he was often unruly, even joking about shooting jurors, a behavior a child psychologist attributed to the false bravado of a scared and overwhelmed child. But there were other moments, away from the prying eyes of others. After the verdict was read, his lawyer recalled that Nathaniel went back to a private room and cried. Later that night, back in the juvenile cell block he shared with other youths accused of violent crimes, he lay on his bunk and cried alone while the others watched an episode of *Law & Order* about a school shooting just like his.

He would spend the rest of his childhood and much of his adult life behind bars, a product of a justice system that had decided he was beyond redemption at the age of thirteen. He will be in his early forties before he is released, a man who has known little else but incarceration since he was a boy. His case prompted an overhaul of the way Florida handles its young violent offenders and became a touchstone in the national debate over juvenile justice. The story of Nathaniel Brazill is a chilling reminder of the devastating consequences of a single, impulsive act of violence. It is the story of a beloved teacher whose life was cut short, of students who lost their innocence in a flash of gunfire, and of a boy who traded the remainder of his youth for a prison cell, his future sealed by a fatal mistake made on the last day of school.

3

A BOTTLE OF LIE

The first known traces of the man who would become the world's greatest wine forger appeared, almost out of thin air, in the early 2000s, under the warm California sun. In Woodland Hills, an outlying district of Los Angeles, a shy, unassuming young man in his early twenties pushed open the door of a renowned local wine shop. He wasn't there to buy wine; he was there to sell a bottle. He was looking for an education, a way into a world of incredible wealth and status. The man, who would eventually be known to the world as Rudy Kurniawan, was a ghost, a chameleon with multiple identities and no verifiable past. But in just a few short years, armed with an almost supernatural palate and an audacious disregard for the truth, he would infiltrate the highest echelons of the fine wine community, perpetrating an international scam of such breathtaking scale that it would take the world's leading experts nearly a decade to bring him down.

The man he met that day in the wine shop was Kyle Smith, a seasoned professional who, for the first time on camera, would later recount the path of the young Asian man who walked into his life. Rudy's request was simple enough. He explained that he had bought a significant amount of 1998 California Cabernet from another merchant, only to discover that it was not a good vintage, and he was hoping to sell the bottles. Smith, seeing a naive but eager young man, agreed. He couldn't have imagined that he was dealing with someone who would one day be sentenced in a New York courtroom for a fraud amounting to tens of millions of dollars.

Beneath his timid exterior, the young Rudy seemed driven by a singular desire: to deepen his knowledge of *Grands Crus*, the great wines of France. His visits to the shop became more frequent, and he peppered the staff with questions. Smith and his colleague, Paul Wasserman, one of California's most renowned wine experts, took the curious young man under their wings. They became his mentors, opening up their encyclopedic knowledge of French wines — their tastes, their grape varieties, their history. It was good timing. In the early 2000s, the American market was dominated by the powerful red wines of Bordeaux, and only a handful of discerning collectors were beginning to bet on the more nuanced and complex wines of Burgundy. Smith and Wasserman encouraged Rudy to venture into this emerging field. They sensed in him a deep-seated need to find something he could excel at, something that would make him important.

Rudy's progress was nothing short of spectacular. In just six months, his palate developed at an astonishing rate. He was a gifted student, a "super taster" with overdeveloped senses and a memory for aroma and flavor that was far beyond average. He would taste, smell, and savor, taking meticulous mental notes to memorize the subtle complexities of every vintage and *Grand Cru* he was introduced to. He had an exceptional memory, learning to identify more than 100 distinct appellations of Burgundy by heart. It was a godsend of a talent, a gift he would later exploit with devastating effect. But Rudy's curiosity extended beyond the contents of the bottle. He questioned his mentors relentlessly about the market for these great French vintages, searching for the unrecognized gems that could be turned into a fortune.

As the American market began its slow pivot from Bordeaux to Burgundy, Rudy understood that this new trend could be incredibly lucrative. To capitalize on it, he needed to immerse himself in the world of those who appreciated these rare beverages. He asked his friend Kyle Smith to introduce him to his exclusive tasting club. The group, known as the "Burg Hounds," comprised twelve of the top wine tasters in Los Angeles, connoisseurs who would meet in the city's finest restaurants to share and critique rare bottles. It was here that the timid young prodigy took his first steps into the closed and rarefied world of the city's finest palates.

From his very first tasting, Rudy was a sensation. In the club's traditional game of blind tasting, the self-taught newcomer, with no formal oenological training, came dangerously close to perfection, consistently identifying wines with an accuracy that stunned the seasoned experts around him. He became an obsessive perfectionist, visiting the wine shop in Woodland Hills daily, tasting everything he could, and beginning to build an impressive wine cellar of his own. These bottles were stored in his modest home in Arcadia, a quiet residential neighborhood north of Los Angeles, where he lived with his mother. It was a place he seemed determined to keep private; Kyle Smith was the only one of his new acquaintances who was ever invited there.

Smith would later recall the strange visit. After having dinner in Rudy's predominantly Chinese neighborhood, Rudy invited him back to the house for a drink. As they approached the front door, Rudy stopped him. "Dude," he said, "when you come into the house, don't freak out when you see what wines I have in there, because my mom thinks they're all $20 or less." Smith was surprised, but he went inside and shared a couple of bottles with his friend. He saw no reason to suspect anything was amiss. But he did realize one thing: the bottles in that house did not cost $20. The average price was closer to $400 or $500 a bottle. In his very first year of collecting, the quiet, unemployed twenty-five-year-old had amassed a collection worth a small fortune, likely around half a million dollars.

The question that hung over Rudy was as potent and unspoken as the aroma of a fine vintage: where was all the money coming from? He was intensely private about his personal life, and he intentionally kept the source of his wealth shrouded in mystery. He told Kyle Smith that his family was involved in liquor distribution in Hong Kong and Indonesia. To others, he presented himself as a "trust fund baby," claiming his wealthy family had essentially exiled him to California, providing him with a million dollars a month to spend as long as he stayed there. His backstory was a shifting narrative of contradictions; at times he was an

Indonesian annuitant who had come to the U.S. to study, other times a political exile, other times an aspiring professional golfer. His history was shaky and confused, but in the intoxicating world of high-end wine, where wealth and eccentricity often went hand-in-hand, no one seemed to worry about it. As his lawyer, Jerome Mooney, would later maintain, the story, at least in its broad strokes, was true. The family had money, and they had sent millions to Rudy.

With a seemingly bottomless well of cash at his disposal, Rudy quickly became a dominant and indispensable figure at wine auctions, the arena where the world's wealthiest connoisseurs competed for the rarest bottles. He stood out, employing a killer technique to intimidate his opponents. He would raise his bidding paddle and simply refuse to put it down, automatically outbidding anyone who challenged him until the wine was his. Witnesses from those early sales remember a compelling, relentless young man who, despite being a newcomer, was impossible to ignore. "Who's this guy?" people would whisper, as he spent lavishly, building a collection that was soon being touted as the greatest in California. He even gave his cellar a name: "Magic." In just two years, he had made his name in the wine world, and this was only the beginning.

The turning point that would transform him from a high-rolling collector to a master forger came with his acquaintance with a certain John Kapon, a young, ambitious New York auctioneer barely older than him. The relationship was symbiotic. Kapon, the head of a renowned auction house called Acker Merrall & Condit, began writing effusive emails about the magnificent and rare wines that Rudy would bring to their tastings. Rudy, in turn, understood that through Kapon, he could turn his passion into a massive business. He wanted to become the biggest and most important dealer in history, but to do that, he had to leave Los Angeles. The world's largest auction houses, the ones breaking all the records, were in Manhattan.

In the winter of 2003, at the age of twenty-seven, Rudy flew to New York. The city's wine market was booming. Between 2002 and 2007, the market for rare wine tripled, from 90 million to 300 million dollars. On the tables of the most luxurious restaurants, *Grands Crus* were a must-have status symbol for a new generation of young, wealthy collectors. Tasting clubs formed one after another, each more exclusive and extravagant than the last. Rudy, with John Kapon as his guide, set his sights on this golden youth of Manhattan. He managed to integrate himself into what was probably the wealthiest and most ostentatious tasting group in the city: the "Twelve Angry Men."

This group of twelve wealthy men in their thirties competed weekly to see who could spend the most on rare wine, adopting superhero nicknames like "Big Boy" and "The Punisher." Rudy chose a pseudonym for himself as well, becoming "Dr. Conti" in reference to his favorite wine, the Domaine de la Romanée-Conti, the most expensive and sought-after in the world. Their parties were Dionysian spectacles of excess. Jeroboams — large-format bottles — of Romanée-Conti would be poured around, and members would be told to dump out their glasses of one priceless wine because an even more prestigious one was on its way. They bragged indecently about their exploits online, posting photos of the bottles like trophies. Rudy quickly adapted their gestures, imitated their mannerisms, and copied their flashy dress codes, driving Lamborghinis and wearing white leather jackets. The once-shy young man from Arcadia slipped effortlessly into the skin of a wealthy, arrogant high-roller, and in just one year, he had not only integrated himself into the group but had also become its leader. His technique for retaining power was simple: he brought increasingly rare and astounding bottles to their dinners, wines that none of the other members had ever seen before.

It was during this time that Rudy developed a peculiar obsession that should have set off alarm bells. After each extravagant tasting, he would insist on having all the empty bottles returned to him. He would instruct the sommeliers to wash them clean, being careful not to damage the labels, and then FedEx them to his home in Arcadia. If a bottle was broken in transit, he would fly into a rage. These empty bottles, these "corpses," were the key to his entire operation. While he was playing the part of a wealthy playboy in New York, he was secretly operating a sophisticated counterfeiting workshop out of his mother's kitchen in Los Angeles.

His method, as later uncovered by fraud expert Michael Egan, was both simple and brilliant. He would take the authentic empty bottles and, using a funnel, refill them with a carefully crafted blend of other, cheaper wines. It was here that his incredible palate and olfactory memory became his most valuable tools. Like a three-star chef with his own secret recipes, he knew exactly which combination of Californian wines, when mixed in the right proportions, could perfectly replicate the taste, color, and aroma of the world's greatest vintages. After filling the bottles, he would turn his attention to the labels. Using photocopying and editing software, the perfectionist would meticulously recreate the labels of the oldest and rarest wines, then artificially age them by baking them in the oven or treating them with liquids to achieve the perfect degree of antiquity. The final, crucial step was the cork. Using a special two-pronged corkscrew, he could remove and reinsert corks without piercing them. A bit of wax around the seal, and the illusion was perfect. In late 2005, after months of perfecting his craft and testing his creations on his unsuspecting acolytes, he was finally ready to launch his global scam.

In 2006, with the help of John Kapon, Rudy organized two anthological sales at Acker Merrall & Condit, which he called "The Cellar" and "The Cellar II." The events were a sensation, drawing the entire elite of the wine world — the most influential critics and the biggest collectors — all eager to get a piece of Kurniawan's legendary "Magic Cellar." He put more than 12,000 bottles up for sale, each one rarer than the next. But some of the offerings were too exceptional to be true. He was selling multiple bottles of wines like the 1945 Romanée-Conti, a vintage of which only 600 bottles were ever produced, the vast majority of which had been consumed decades earlier. The estate's own manager said he had never seen a bottle of it in his life, yet Rudy had several. Despite these glaring incongruities, the plan worked perfectly. The sales grossed a staggering $35 million, a historic record, with the vast majority of the wines sold being fake.

The first real doubts began to surface a few months later, as collectors began to open their expensive purchases. One of Douglas Banzle's friends, a major buyer at the auctions, held a tasting of eleven of his newly acquired wines. Six of them were clearly fake. The whispers had begun, but Rudy continued his unscrupulous business. The mistake that would finally lead to his downfall came in April 2008, at another auction offering several lots from Rudy's cellar. Douglas Banzle, the Burgundy expert, was perusing the catalog when he saw something that stopped him cold: several lots of very old Clos Saint-Denis from the esteemed Domaine Ponsot, with vintages from the 1940s, '50s, and '60s. His first thought was one of excitement; he had never seen those before. His second thought was one of suspicion: he had never seen them before because Domaine Ponsot had not started producing that particular wine until 1982.

Banzle immediately emailed Domaine's owner, Laurent Ponsot, in Burgundy. Ponsot, who had never heard of Rudy Kurniawan, was stunned. He called the auction house and spoke to John Kapon, who dismissively told him that the bottles had all been authenticated by experts. When Ponsot revealed who he was and insisted the wines were fake, Kapon reluctantly agreed to withdraw them from the sale but Ponsot was not convinced. He jumped on the next plane to New York and arrived just in time for the auction, where he discovered that Rudy was offering nearly 100 bottles from his domain, almost all of them fakes, with an estimated value of over a million dollars. Kapon was forced to publicly announce the withdrawal of the lots at Ponsot's request.

The next day, Ponsot arranged a lunch meeting with Rudy, Kapon, and Banzle. When Ponsot asked where the fake bottles had come from, Rudy and Kapon mumbled that they couldn't recall, that they bought so much wine it was impossible to keep track. At that moment, Ponsot knew that Rudy was hiding something. The man who had been described to him as cheerful and urbane was withdrawn, reserved, and haughty. From that day forward, Laurent Ponsot began his own private, two-year investigation, a "Don Quixote"-like quest that took him all over the world, chasing down leads and uncovering evidence of Rudy's massive counterfeiting operation.

Meanwhile, the Federal Bureau of Investigation (FBI), led by prosecutor Jason Hernandez, had also begun to take an interest in Rudy Kurniawan. Their investigation eventually overlapped with Ponsot's, and they joined forces, pooling their research. The evidence they accumulated was damning. The FBI finally had enough to bring him down. On the morning of March 8, 2012, they raided Rudy's home in Arcadia. What they found inside was worthy of a crime film. The house was a counterfeiting factory. The kitchen had been transformed into a laboratory with its windows covered to conceal the activity. Wine-making utensils and empty bottles soaking in the sink were everywhere. In drawers, they found 19,000 fake labels for the world's twenty-seven best wines, thousands of stamps with the logos of the biggest domaines, and hundreds of authentic-looking corks. Rudy Kurniawan, surprised and silent, was arrested on the spot.

His trial began in New York in December 2013. After twenty months behind bars, the man who appeared in court looked nothing like the flamboyant high-roller he had once been. He had lost a significant amount of weight and was calm and silent. But as the trial progressed, it became clear he was in a state of complete denial. Dozens of witnesses took the stand, the forged bottles were displayed one by one, but the accused showed no signs of remorse. He would smile and nod at Laurent Ponsot from across the courtroom, seemingly detached from the reality of his situation. He pleaded not guilty. His lawyers, faced with the mountain of evidence found in his home, were left with little to argue. In a moment of courtroom absurdity that drew laughter from the gallery, his lawyer, Jerome Mooney, claimed that the 19,000 fake labels had simply been used to create a decorative wine-themed wallpaper for his new home. On August 8, 2014, the verdict finally fell. Rudy Kurniawan was found guilty and sentenced to ten years in prison. As the sentence was announced, Laurent Ponsot, who was sitting right behind him, saw his shoulders fall, a final, subtle admission that the game was over. He had played to the very end, and he had lost. A complete mystery still remains. Did he have accomplices? And, most disturbingly, how many of the thousands of bottles created by the forger still lie dormant in the cellars of the world's biggest collectors, ticking time bombs of deceit waiting to be uncorked?

4

CIRCLEVILLE LETTERS

Just thirty miles (about forty-eight kilometers) south of Columbus, Ohio, lies the town of Circleville, a place that proudly proclaimed itself "The Best Little Town Around." In the 1970s, it was a small community of roughly 11,000 people, the kind of place where neighbors knew each other and life moved at a steady, predictable rhythm. But beginning in 1977, this seemingly peaceful town, along with the wider region of Southern Ohio, became the target of a relentless campaign of harassment orchestrated by an anonymous figure known only as the Circleville Letter Writer. Over the next two decades, more than a thousand threatening and accusatory letters, written in distinctive block print, would terrorize residents, poison relationships, and ultimately become entangled with suspicion, tragedy, and a mystery that officially remains closed, yet continues to provoke debate.

The campaign began subtly enough on March 2, 1977, with a letter addressed not to a resident of Circleville itself, but to Gordon Massie, the superintendent of the nearby Westfall High School. The letter, penned in block letters that would become the writer's signature, accused Massie of impropriety with female school bus drivers under his supervision. "Dear sir," it began, "according to my girlfriend, you have asked her to go out many times and have asked the other female bus drivers, too. Due to your position and their jobs with you, you should not do this. This must stop at once for the good of this school and families." The writer threatened to escalate the matter to the school board if the alleged behavior continued, invoking a sense of moral righteousness. "To prey on another man's girl is untouchable, especially when they're out trying to make a living," the letter continued, before taking a sharper, more vulgar turn, "There's also talk of you dating a married woman and taking advantage of them... I suggest you find yourself a pimple-faced whore and start up with her and leave my girls alone."

The initial letter set the tone for what was to come: accusations of infidelity and workplace harassment, veiled threats, and a jarring mix of moral condemnation and crude language. The writer clearly believed they were acting as a moral arbiter, exposing perceived wrongs within the community. A few days later, the threats were carried out; a second letter arrived at the school board, demanding an investigation into Massie's conduct. Simultaneously, a third letter containing the same accusations was sent to Massie's fellow superintendent, spreading the allegations further.

Soon, however, the anonymous writer shifted their focus, zeroing in on one particular individual: Mary Gillispie, one of the school bus drivers working under Massie. Mary was a married mother of two, and the letters accused her directly of having an affair with Gordon Massie, who was also married with a family. The tone immediately became more personal and menacing. "Mrs. Gillispie," one of the first letters addressed to her read, "stay away from Massie. Don't lie when questioned about meeting him. I know where you live. I've been observing your house and know you have children. This is no joke. Please take it serious. Everyone concerned has been notified and everything will be over soon."

The writer seemed obsessed with exposing this alleged affair, positioning themselves as a defender of marital fidelity while simultaneously employing tactics of fear and intimidation. Another letter dripped with contempt, stating bluntly, "Lady, this is your last chance to report him. I know you are a pig and will prove it and shame you out of Ohio. A pig sneaks around and meets other women's husbands behind their backs. It causes families and homes and marriages to suffer." Despite Mary's consistent denials of any affair, the letters continued, flooding her life with anonymous accusations and growing threats.

The harassment soon expanded to target Mary's husband, Ronald Gillispie. Letters arrived informing him of his wife's alleged infidelity with Massie. More disturbingly, the writer began actively inciting violence, recommending that Ron catch Mary and Gordon in the act and kill them, stating that Massie "doesn't deserve to live." When Ron didn't act on these gruesome suggestions, the letters turned threatening toward him as well, demonstrating a chilling knowledge of his personal life, detailing the car he drove and the school his children attended. Ron, deeply disturbed, took the letters to the Pickaway County Sheriff, Dwight Radcliffe. However, according to Ron's brother-in-law, Paul Freshour, the sheriff dismissed Ron's concerns, stating he had more important matters to deal with. It seemed that the authorities offered no immediate recourse against the anonymous tormentor.

The campaign escalated beyond mailed threats. Obscene, crudely made signs began appearing around Circleville, plastered in public spaces for all to see. These signs repeated the accusations against Mary Gillispie and Gordon Massie, but some took a horrifyingly personal turn, describing vile sexual acts supposedly occurring between Massie and the Gillispies' young eight-year-old daughter. According to Paul Freshour, Ron Gillispie became consumed by the need to protect his family's reputation and shield his children from these disgusting public displays. Freshour claimed that Ron began a daily ritual, driving around town for an hour or two before work each morning to find and tear down the signs that had inevitably popped up overnight. The anonymous writer was not just sending letters; they were actively engaging in a public shaming campaign, forcing the Gillispie family into a state of constant vigilance and fear.

The Gillispies, according to Paul Freshour, believed they knew who was behind the relentless harassment. On the night of August 19, 1977, about five months after the first letter was sent, the situation reached a tragic climax. Mary was away, traveling to Florida with her sister-in-law (Ron's sister), Karen Sue Freshour, and some friends. Around 10:00 p.m., Ron received a phone call at home. The contents of that call remain unknown, but whatever Ron heard seemed to confirm his suspicions about the identity of the person tormenting his family. He allegedly told his young daughter that he was going to confront the culprit. He then took his gun, got into his truck, and drove off into the night.

Just ten minutes from his home, on a rural road called Five Points Pike, Ron Gillispie crashed his car into a tree. He hit the tree at 10:25 p.m. Not wearing a seatbelt, he was partially ejected from the vehicle and is believed to have died on impact. He was officially pronounced dead upon arrival at the hospital at 11:15 p.m. Ron was only thirty-five years old. The weather conditions that night were clear, though the road would have been dark. The official coroner's report ruled his death an accident, noting that he had been traveling at excessive speed and missed a curve in the road. A pathology report also revealed his blood alcohol content was 0.16, double the legal limit at the time.

However, Ron's brother-in-law, Paul Freshour, contested the official findings. He insisted that Ron, who he claimed rarely drank heavily, was wildly out of character to be driving drunk. Freshour alleged that Ron hadn't simply crashed but had actually been involved in a high-speed chase, claiming there were bullet holes in the side of the truck. Despite Freshour's urging the sheriff's office to investigate further, no evidence was ever found to support his claims of foul play. The official ruling remained an accident caused by speeding and alcohol impairment.

Ron Gillispie's death did nothing to deter the Circleville Letter Writer; if anything, it seemed to embolden them. New letters emerged, now accusing Mary Gillispie and Gordon Massie of murdering Ron. The writer even claimed that Sheriff Dwight Radcliffe himself was involved in covering up the supposed murder to protect Gordon Massie. Adding another layer of complexity and suspicion to the narrative, Mary Gillispie, who had vehemently denied the affair with Gordon Massie before her husband's death, began a public relationship with Massie afterward. Gordon Massie and his wife eventually divorced, with his wife citing "extreme cruelty" as one of the reasons. While this sequence of events didn't prove the writer's initial accusations, it certainly fueled local gossip and lent a disturbing credence to the idea that there might have been some truth underlying the anonymous harassment.

The threats against Mary continued unabated for years. Then, on the afternoon of February 7, 1983, nearly six years after Ron's death, the writer attempted to escalate their campaign from psychological torment to physical violence. Mary was driving her school bus route, about to turn onto the very same street where her husband had fatally crashed. She spotted yet another sign, this one bearing an obscene message about her daughter, who was now thirteen-years-old. Fed up, Mary stopped the bus, got out, and went to remove the sign, which was crudely attached to a fence. As she pulled at it, she noticed it was connected by twine to a small, nondescript box resting nearby. Apparently not recognizing the potential danger, she detached the sign and took the box home with her. Inside, she found a loaded .25-caliber pistol.

When Mary brought the box containing the gun to Sheriff Radcliffe, the authorities immediately recognized it for what it was: a potentially lethal booby trap that had miraculously failed to detonate. According to the sheriff, the mechanism was designed so that the gun would fire if someone simply tried to rip the sign off the fence. Because Mary had instead removed the entire box along with the sign, the trigger mechanism wasn't activated. The gun itself offered a crucial lead. Its serial number had been crudely filed off, but technicians at the Bureau of Criminal Investigations lab were able to recover it. The number was traced back to a man in Columbus, Ohio. When questioned, the man stated that he had sold the pistol to his coworker and direct supervisor at the local Anheuser-Busch facility: Paul Freshour, Mary Gillispie's brother-in-law, the same man who had been vocal about his suspicions surrounding Ron Gillispie's death.

Suddenly, Paul Freshour, who had been a seemingly peripheral figure offering commentary, became the prime suspect. When confronted by police, Freshour admitted to buying the gun in December 1982, just a few months before Mary discovered it. He claimed he had purchased it for protection because his own wife and children were being harassed. However, he asserted that the gun had been stolen from his garage sometime before the booby trap incident. Despite this claim, he had never reported the gun missing to the police. Adding to the suspicion, he told investigators he knew who had stolen it but refused to name the person. Freshour otherwise cooperated fully with the investigation, allowing searches of his home and car, providing handwriting samples, waiving his right to an attorney, and even agreeing to take a polygraph test. He subsequently failed the polygraph.

The case against Paul Freshour intensified dramatically when his estranged wife, Karen Sue, came forward and told police that Paul was, in fact, the anonymous Circleville letter writer. Paul and Karen Sue were married for twenty years before divorcing in October 1982, during which Paul allegedly abused her and accused her of cheating — echoing the same themes found in the letters. Karen Sue claimed she had discovered evidence of his letter-writing years earlier. She recounted finding pieces of a torn-up letter mentioning the name "Gillispie" in a toilet and finding several other similar letters hidden around the house. She also claimed to have found four letters in the trunk of Paul's car shortly after Ron's death, which Paul allegedly told her Ron had wanted him to mail. A coworker of Karen Sue corroborated parts of her story, confirming to police that Karen Sue had previously mentioned finding letters in her home written in the same block style as the notorious Circleville letters. Paul Freshour vehemently denied his ex-wife's accusations, maintaining his innocence regarding both the letters and the booby trap, and suggested that Karen Sue was attempting to set him up.

While Paul Freshour was the main focus, other potential suspects were briefly considered. Paul himself had apparently suspected his and Karen Sue's adult son, Mark Freshour, of stealing the gun from the garage, though friends claimed Paul would never have implicated his own son to the police. Another theory pointed to William Massie, Gordon Massie's son. He would have been in his late teens or early twenties when the letters started, potentially angered by his parents' impending divorce, for which his mother cited "extreme cruelty." Some later letters were even reportedly signed "Bill Massie," but skepticism remained about his ability to orchestrate the campaign while still living under his father's roof.

Despite the lack of direct physical evidence connecting him to the booby trap and his corroborated alibi for much of the time the trap would have been set, Paul Freshour was arrested and tried for attempted murder in October 1983. He pleaded not guilty. Although he was not formally charged in connection with the letters, the judge allowed thirty-nine of the anonymous missives to be presented as evidence during the trial. The prosecution argued that the handwriting on the chalk box containing the booby trap (an industrial chalk box potentially sourced from Paul's workplace at Anheuser-Busch) was similar to the writing in the letters. Two document examiners testified that the handwriting in the letters *could* have been Freshour's, though it wasn't a definitive match. After deliberating for only two and a half hours, the jury found Paul Freshour guilty of attempted murder. He was sentenced to the maximum term of seven to twenty-five years in prison. Although never proven in court, most people in the community now assumed he was indeed the Circleville Letter Writer.

The conviction, however, did not bring an end to the harassment. In a baffling turn of events, the letters continued, even intensified, while Paul Freshour was incarcerated nearly 100 miles (about 160 kilometers) away in Lima, Ohio. Hundreds more letters were sent during his decade behind bars. The prison warden stated unequivocally that it would have been impossible for Freshour to have written and mailed them from inside. He was kept in isolation, denied access to pens and paper, and all his incoming and outgoing mail was meticulously inspected. Furthermore, the letters continued to be postmarked from Columbus, Ohio, far from the prison. Authorities clung to the theory that Freshour must have had an accomplice on the outside mailing letters on his behalf. The ongoing letters were cited as the reason for his parole denial after seven years. Shortly after the denial, Freshour himself received a taunting letter in prison: "Freshour, now when are you going to believe you aren't getting out of there? I told you two years ago when we set 'em up. They stay set up... No one wants you out... The joke is on you. Ha ha."

The letters finally, abruptly stopped in 1994, the same year Paul Freshour was released from prison after serving ten years. Upon his release, he reportedly contacted the FBI, asking them to investigate the case and clear his name, but received no response. Paul Freshour died in 2012 at the age of seventy, maintaining his innocence to the very end. His son, Mark, who never visited him in prison, died by apparent suicide in 2002.

Despite the glaring questions surrounding the letters sent during Paul's imprisonment, the Pickaway County Sheriff's Office officially considers the case of the Circleville letters closed. Recent investigations by the podcast "Whatever Remains" and the television show *48 Hours* have also concluded that Paul Freshour was the sole perpetrator, somehow managing the letters from prison or having an accomplice. Yet, the identity of a potential accomplice, if one existed, has never been discovered, nor has a definitive explanation been offered for how Freshour could have orchestrated the continued campaign from within the confines of prison. After his release, the Circleville letters stopped, but questions remained — was one man really behind the years of harassment, or does the mystery still hide unanswered truths?

5

THE BONES ON THE MESA

On the evening of February 2, 2009, during a routine walk, a married couple's dog unearthed something unusual sticking out of the sandy soil. Unsure what it was but suspecting the worst, the wife snapped a photo and sent it to her sister, a nurse. The immediate response confirmed their fears: the bone was almost certainly human. They called the authorities, having no idea that this single, protruding bone was merely the first fragment of a nightmare that had lain buried beneath the desert surface for years, a discovery that would expose a horrific series of crimes and reveal a chilling indifference to the lives of some of the city's most vulnerable women.

What the couple had stumbled upon was initially believed to be a single femur or hip bone. Authorities began a careful excavation, expecting to perhaps uncover the rest of a single skeleton. But by February 10th, the scope of the discovery had exploded. They hadn't found one body; they had unearthed the partial remains of three separate individuals. It was sickeningly clear: this was not an isolated burial; it was a mass grave. The realization sent shockwaves through the Albuquerque Police Department and the wider community. Specialists were called in from across the region to assist in the painstaking task of sifting through the disturbed earth.

The location presented immense challenges. The plot had already been significantly disrupted by the heavy machinery used by previous developers who had begun construction before abandoning the project. Investigators knew the bodies could have been buried long before construction started, meaning the developers might have unknowingly unearthed, scattered, and reburied skeletal fragments across the vast site. This was a terrifying thought; keeping the crime scene intact and making sure all the remains were found and correctly matched seemed nearly impossible. Furthermore, the discovery of multiple bodies immediately raised the specter of a serial killer, making the careful collection of any potential trace evidence paramount.

A large-scale operation commenced. Heavy equipment was brought in, but instead of digging aggressively, it was used to slowly move large piles of dirt, which were then meticulously sifted by hand. Cadaver dogs, satellite maps, and ground-penetrating radar were employed to help pinpoint potential burial locations without further disturbing the site. The process was tedious and grim. Some skeletons were found relatively intact, buried as deep as eight feet (about 2.5 meters) below the surface, while others were mere inches down, their bones scattered haphazardly, stark evidence of the construction activity that had churned the earth above them. All the remains found were skeletal; decomposition was complete, leaving only bones. Most were discovered without any clothing or personal items that could aid in identification. Determining the cause of death and simply figuring out who these individuals were would be monumental challenges. As remains were located, their positions were carefully mapped before being handed over to medical examiners.

The first identification came quickly. On February 11th, just a day after the discovery of the third body, dental records confirmed one set of remains belonged to twenty-six-year-old Victoria Chavez. She had been reported missing in March 2005, though her family hadn't actually seen her for nearly a year prior to that report. Like many of the women who would eventually be identified, Victoria had struggled with drug addiction and was involved in sex work. At the time of her disappearance, she was on probation. Her skeletal remains were found relatively close to the surface, buried only about eighteen inches (about forty-five centimeters) deep, suggesting they had likely been disturbed by the construction work. No clothing or identifying items were found with her body.

The grim discoveries continued. By February 18th, the total number of individuals found had risen to six. Victoria Chavez's complete skeletal remains were finally pieced together that day, making her the fourth full set recovered; the other two were still missing significant portions. The destructive impact of the earlier digging was becoming painfully evident. Just six days later, on February 24th, the number climbed again, reaching a staggering ten sets of remains. The Albuquerque Police Department, realizing the scale and complexity of the case, formally requested assistance from the FBI and brought in archaeologists from the University of New Mexico to aid in the recovery and analysis. Profilers were consulted, trying to build a picture of the person, almost certainly a serial killer, who was responsible for this horror.

Among the ten sets of remains was one that held a particularly heartbreaking secret. Inside the pelvic bones of one skeleton lay the tiny, fragile bones of a fetus. The woman had been pregnant when she was killed, estimated to be about four months along. Dental records eventually provided a name: twenty-two-year-old Gina Michelle Valdez, known to her loved ones simply as Michelle. Her father remembered her as a kind, giving person who would give you the shirt off her back, and as an amazing mother to the young daughter she already had. She had dreams of becoming a singer or a lawyer, aspirations tragically cut short when she fell into a life of drug addiction she couldn't escape. Her family described a painful pattern: she would disappear for days, then weeks, then months at a time. She would occasionally call her father, usually asking for money, and each time he would plead with her to come home, giving her the money in the desperate hope it might encourage her return. Then, the calls stopped altogether. He reported her missing in February 2005. Shortly after, rumors began to circulate — rumors that Michelle's mother later reported hearing from numerous sources — that Michelle had been stabbed multiple times and her body dumped somewhere on the West Mesa, precisely where she was ultimately found. Disturbingly similar rumors would surface regarding other victims, leads provided by desperate families that were tragically, and perhaps negligently, never adequately pursued by law enforcement at the time.

By February 28th, the final count was reached: eleven adult bodies and one fetus had been unearthed from the makeshift desert graveyard. The third victim to be identified, again through dental records, was thirty-two-year-old Cinnamon Elks. The oldest of the victims found, Cinnamon also struggled with addiction and sex work, primarily in an area of Albuquerque known colloquially as the "War Zone," where most of the victims were known to frequent. She had a lengthy criminal record filled with drug and solicitation charges and led such a transient lifestyle that pinpointing the exact time of her disappearance was difficult. The last confirmed sighting was her arrest in July 2004. When her birthday arrived in August and she failed to make her customary call to her family, they knew something was wrong and tried to report her missing. Initially, police were dismissive, telling her mother that Cinnamon was a grown adult who didn't need to check in. It took until December, months later, for a formal missing person report to be filed. Just like Michelle Valdez's family, Cinnamon's mother also heard chilling rumors. Friends from Cinnamon's circle reported that just before she disappeared, she had spoken fearfully of a "dirty cop" who was picking up sex workers, killing them, and burying them on the West Mesa. This was now the second distinct report mentioning abduction, murder, and disposal in West Mesa, yet these warnings seem to have gone unheeded.

The fourth identification was twenty-four-year-old Julie Nieto, a young mother remembered by her family as caring and well-behaved before drug addiction took hold when she was nineteen. Despite her struggles, she desperately wanted to get clean for her son, making multiple attempts at rehabilitation. Even when she was unable to care for him, she maintained contact, visiting him and bringing presents whenever she could. She was reported missing in August 2004, shortly after Cinnamon Elks was last seen. As with the others, her disappearance was not treated with urgency. A significant connection emerged as these first four women were identified: they all knew each other. This wasn't entirely surprising, given they moved in the same dangerous circles of addiction and sex work in the War Zone. Investigators hoped this link might provide a clue, a reason why these specific women were targeted, but it offered little immediate direction.

In early April 2009, two more victims were named. Twenty-two-year-old Monica Candelaria was remembered as someone always laughing, who adored her family and children. She was last seen on May 11, 2003, and reported missing just two weeks later, making her one of the earliest disappearances connected to the site. Once again, rumors surfaced shortly after she vanished. Friends, including a neighbor named Isaac, told her family they heard Monica had been killed and buried on the West Mesa — the third instance of this specific rumor being reported years before the bodies were found. In Monica's case, there is evidence that investigators did initially follow up on these leads, but the trail went cold, and her case was eventually relegated to the cold case unit. The sixth victim identified was twenty-six-year-old Veronica Romero. She was reported missing by her family on Valentine's Day, 2004.

The large number of remains and their fragmented condition made it necessary to bring in additional experts. Boxes of bones were sent to the Center for Human Identification in Denton, Texas, for advanced DNA analysis, while forensic anthropologists worked tirelessly on-site and in labs to piece together the human puzzle. The task force, now numbering around forty individuals, expanded their search, contacting law enforcement agencies in neighboring states like Arizona and Texas, and even as far as Milwaukee, looking for similar patterns, other serial killers who targeted sex workers, hoping to find a connection.

Soon after, the seventh victim was identified: twenty-four-year-old Doreen Marquez. Her story stood out. Unlike many of the others, Doreen grew up in West Mesa itself, attended West Mesa High School (less than a mile from her eventual burial site), was a cheerleader, and got good grades. She had two children, lived in a nice house, and was known for her style and sassy personality. Her life took a sharp downturn when her boyfriend was incarcerated. Having never previously been involved with drugs or sex work, she suddenly spiraled, leaving her children with family and disappearing for increasingly long periods. The exact date she went missing is disputed; her family last saw her in October 2003, while friends claimed to have seen her in early 2004. She was formally reported missing in December 2004. Although she had no criminal record related to sex work, it was widely assumed she had become involved due to her association with the other victims and the War Zone.

Crucially, all seven victims identified up to this point were Hispanic, local to Albuquerque, and every single one of them had been on the list compiled years earlier by Detective Ida Lopez, the cold case detective whose warnings about a potential serial killer targeting vulnerable women had been largely ignored. Her list, tragically accurate, now became a vital tool for investigators trying to speed up the identification process.

However, one set of remains didn't fit the pattern. They belonged to a Black female, estimated to be in her mid-teens, who didn't match any missing person reports from the Albuquerque area. Clues found with her body included an acrylic fingernail with a very specific, unique design. Police circulated sketches and details — that she had suffered a broken nose and an unrelated stab wound at some point in her life — hoping someone would recognize her. By November 2009, the remains were formally identified as fifteen-year-old Syllannia Edwards, the eighth victim. Syllannia had been in the foster care system since age five, after both her parents were imprisoned. She had run away from her foster home in Lawton, Oklahoma, at some point, though exactly when she was reported missing is unclear. The prevailing theory is that she fell in with a group traveling the I-40 corridor, engaging in sex work to survive. A tip placed her at a hotel in Denver in 2004, after which it's believed she made her way south to New Mexico, where she met her end.

Shortly after Syllannia's identification came the ninth and tenth victims. Twenty-four-year-old Virginia Cloven was remembered as having a hilarious and unique personality, doing well in school while always making people laugh. Her life took a tragic turn when her brother was murdered. Devastated, Virginia, then seventeen, ran away from home, followed shortly after by her other brother. After a brief stay with her grandfather, she moved in with a boyfriend, only to face further tragedy when he was hit by a car and fell into a coma. Homeless and traumatized, she ended up in the War Zone. She maintained sporadic contact with her father, who tried desperately to help her. In June 2004, she called him, sounding enthusiastic, claiming she had met someone she planned to marry and that her life was turning around. Almost immediately after that hopeful call, she vanished completely. She was reported missing four months later.

The final two victims were identified together: Twenty-three-year-old Evelyn Salazar and her fifteen-year-old cousin, Jamie Barela. Evelyn, like most of the others, was involved in drugs and sex work. On a day in late March or early April 2004, after spending time with her family, Evelyn offered to take Jamie to a park located just outside the War Zone. Neither of them ever returned, being reported missing together on April 3rd. Jamie Barela was the tragic anomaly among the victims; she had no involvement in drugs or sex work. She was simply in the wrong place at the wrong time, likely killed because she was with Evelyn when the killer struck. Her death led to speculation that the killer might have known his victims, perhaps targeting Evelyn and killing Jamie only because she witnessed it, or that he viewed any young woman in the War Zone as a sex worker and therefore expendable.

With all eleven victims identified, the grim task of finding their killer intensified, hampered by a near total lack of forensic evidence. No clear cause of death could be determined for any of the victims, though the absence of stab or gunshot wounds led investigators to believe strangulation or suffocation was the likely method. The burial site yielded no foreign DNA, no fibers, no definitive clues linking anyone to the disposal of the bodies. By July 2009, authorities announced they had narrowed their focus to a handful of suspects.

One early person of interest was Ron Erwin, a photographer from Joplin, Missouri, who frequented the New Mexico State Fair near the burial site. A search of his home uncovered thousands of disturbing photographs depicting women posed as if they were dead. While shocking, all the women in the photos were later found alive and well. Erwin cooperated fully, even taking a polygraph, and alibis confirmed he wasn't in Albuquerque during some of the disappearances, leading investigators to largely rule him out.

Another suspect was Fred Reynolds, a local pimp known to associate with several of the victims. He had actively sought information about the missing women from their families, raising initial suspicion. However, Reynolds died of natural causes just a month before the remains were discovered. Family members told police his inquiries stemmed from genuine concern, not morbid curiosity.

Two suspects, however, emerged as far more compelling possibilities. Lorenzo Montoya lived in a trailer just about two miles (three kilometers) from the mass grave. He had a significant history of violence against women and soliciting sex workers. In 1998, police intervened when they caught him attempting to kill a sex worker he had lured to a dead-end road; the case was later dismissed. Crucially, Montoya was killed in December 2006 — around the exact time the disappearances linked to the West Mesa site stopped. He was shot by a pimp, Frederick Williams, while attempting to dispose of the body of nineteen-year-old Shericka Hill, whom he had raped and strangled in his trailer. The method matched the suspected cause of death for the West Mesa victims. Even more damning, satellite images taken between 2003 and 2006 showed tire tracks leading directly from the remote burial site back to Montoya's trailer. A disturbing videotape was also found in his trailer, seemingly recorded at the end of an encounter with a sex worker; while nothing explicit is seen or heard, the distinct sounds of duct tape and a trash bag being handled are audible — items Montoya used when disposing of Shericka Hill's belongings. Despite this mountain of circumstantial evidence, no DNA linked Montoya directly to the West Mesa crime scene, and his death left investigators unable to question him.

The final prime suspect was Joseph Blea. His ex-wife tipped off police shortly after the bodies were found, stating that he frequently visited sex workers but also expressed intense hatred toward them, and that he often dumped trash in the specific West Mesa area where the remains were discovered. Blea had an extensive criminal record, with nearly 140 police contacts between 1990 and 2009, including arrests for breaking into homes to steal women's underwear and jewelry, indecent exposure, and attempted kidnapping of a sex worker. Police surveillance confirmed his ex-wife's claims; he would drive through the War Zone multiple times a day, not soliciting, but slowly cruising and intently watching the women working there. A search of his home uncovered collections of women's underwear and jewelry, potentially connecting him to items reported missing from some of the victims. The strongest physical evidence connecting Blea to the site was a small plastic tree tag, bought from a nursery he often visited between 2003 and 2006 — the same period as the murders. This tag was found buried eight feet (about 2.5 meters) deep, directly with one set of skeletal remains. While highly suspicious, authorities couldn't definitively prove how the tag got there; it could potentially have been moved during construction or discarded as trash, as his ex-wife suggested. Blea was eventually arrested and convicted for a series of unrelated home invasion sexual assaults on middle school-aged children from the 80s and 90s, as well as the murder of another sex worker from the War Zone, linked by DNA. According to a cellmate, while incarcerated, Blea spoke constantly and disparagingly about the West Mesa victims, calling them "trashy" but knowing all their names and admitting to having paid some for sex and hitting at least one of them.

Despite the strong circumstantial cases against Montoya and Blea, the West Mesa Bone Collector case officially remains unsolved. No charges have ever been filed due to the lack of definitive forensic evidence connecting any single individual to all eleven murders. The tragedy spurred community action, including protests demanding better police attention to crimes against marginalized women and the formation of Safe Streets New Mexico by a survivor of another infamous killer, aimed at protecting sex workers. For the families of the victims, the pain lingers, compounded by the knowledge that the system failed to protect them and has yet to bring their killer, or killers, to justice. Authorities still believe other victims may be buried elsewhere, women who disappeared during the same timeframe, their names adding to the haunting list of the forgotten.

6

GLORIAVALE CHRISTIAN COMMUNITY

On March 26, 1997, a former member of a reclusive religious group named Rio D'Angelo received a package in the mail. Inside were letters and videotapes indicating that the members of the group, known as Heaven's Gate, had committed mass suicide. Following the instructions included in the package, D'Angelo drove to the sprawling mansion the cult rented in the affluent San Diego suburb of Rancho Santa Fe. What he found there, and filmed as instructed, was a scene of eerie, meticulously staged death that would soon shock the nation and the world. Thirty-nine bodies lay peacefully in bunk beds and on mattresses throughout the house, all dressed in identical black uniforms and black-and-white Nike sneakers, their faces and torsos covered with purple shrouds. It was the quiet, orderly culmination of a bizarre journey that began over two decades earlier, a journey led by a charismatic former music professor and a nurse who believed they were extraterrestrial beings sent to lead humanity to salvation aboard a UFO. The Heaven's Gate cult operated for years in near-total seclusion, stripping its members of their identities not through violence or overt coercion, but through a gradual, insidious process of psychological manipulation, preparing them for a final "graduation" from their human existence.

The story of Heaven's Gate is linked to the life of its co-founder, Marshall Herff Applewhite Jr., born on May 17, 1931, in Spur, Texas. He went by his middle name, Herff, in his youth. His upbringing was steeped in religion; his father, Marshall Herff Applewhite Sr., was a Presbyterian minister who moved the family frequently around South Texas, establishing new churches every few years. While outwardly Herff Sr. and his wife, Louise, were seen as kind and devoted parents, some family members recalled the senior Applewhite as a strict authoritarian, particularly hard on young Herff, whom he pressured relentlessly to follow him into the ministry. Herff Jr. desperately wanted to make his father proud and aspired to become a minister himself from a young age, once walking into his father's church and telling the parishioners that he couldn't wait to preach the word of God one day.

By all accounts, Herff was a charismatic and intelligent child, always smiling and full of life, often described by his sister Louise as the comedian of the family, always able to get everyone laughing. As a teenager at Corpus Christi High School, he blossomed into a tall, good-looking young man with piercing blue eyes, known by his classmates as an outgoing overachiever who was always smiling. After graduating, he enrolled at Austin College, still intending to pursue the ministry. He excelled in college, becoming the leader of the acapella choir and participating in the Judiciary Council before graduating with a degree in philosophy in 1952. That same year, he married his high school girlfriend, Anne Francis Pierce, and enrolled at the Union Theological Seminary of Virginia, seemingly on track to fulfill his father's expectations.

But after only one semester, Herff made a decision that would alter the course of his life. He left the seminary to pursue his true passion: music. He possessed a remarkable singing voice, particularly suited for opera, and he set out on a new path. He and Anne moved to North Carolina, where he took a job as the Director of Music at the First Presbyterian Church. Life seemed good until 1954, when he was drafted into the army. He served for two years, stationed briefly in Austria and then in New Mexico, rising to the rank of sergeant before being honorably discharged in 1956. Upon his return, he immediately enrolled at the University of Colorado to pursue a master's degree in music with an emphasis on musical theater.

There, he became heavily involved in the local theater scene, even acting alongside an eighteen-year-old Joan Van Ark in a community production of *Annie Get Your Gun*.

After graduating, Herff landed a position as a music professor at the University of Alabama in 1959. He quickly became a beloved and respected faculty member, known for his upbeat personality, laid-back teaching style, and ability to captivate students. He and Anne settled into the community, raising their two young children, Mark and Lane. They appeared to have the perfect, idyllic life. But beneath the surface, Herff was hiding a profound internal struggle. In 1965, his carefully constructed world fell apart when Anne suddenly left him, taking the children with her. The reason soon surfaced: Herff had been having an affair with a male graduate student. He had been living a double life, torn between the expectations of his religious upbringing and his own sexuality. Anne filed for divorce, which was finalized in 1968.

The revelation and the subsequent collapse of his marriage marked the beginning of a deep psychological decline for Herff. He left his position at the University of Alabama and moved back to Texas, becoming the chair of the music department at the University of St. Thomas in Houston. He threw himself into his work, becoming deeply involved with the Houston Grand Opera and starring in fifteen productions alongside famous artists like Plácido Domingo, a Spanish opera singer, earning rave reviews. He was at the height of his musical career but the internal conflict continued to fester. Eventually, he gathered the courage to tell his parents he was gay. Their reaction was exactly what he had feared, his strict father reportedly being appalled and asking, "What kind of sins have I committed for the Lord to scorn me this way?" Herff felt utterly rejected, not only by his parents but by the Presbyterian Church that had been the bedrock of his entire life.

He fell into a deep depression, even contemplating suicide by jumping off a bridge. His colleagues noticed a dramatic shift in his personality; the articulate, mild-mannered man they knew became paranoid, agitated, and seemed to have a "perpetual crazed look in his eyes." It was around this time that he began hearing voices and having visions. During a trip to

Galveston beach, he claimed to have received a divine vision revealing the origins and destiny of the human race. Simultaneously, he developed a fervent interest in UFOs and extraterrestrials, a common fascination in the 1960s and '70s, but one that took on a more ominous significance in the context of his deteriorating mental state. By 1970, after suffering several mental breakdowns, Herff was let go from his job at the University of St. Thomas, ostensibly due to "health problems of an emotional nature." The death of his father in 1971 sent him spiraling further.

Everything came to a head in 1972 when Herff was admitted to a hospital in Houston. The exact reason for his admission remains unclear; his sister claimed it was for a near-fatal heart blockage that caused brain damage, cementing his psychosis, while others suggest he voluntarily checked himself into the psychiatric ward seeking a "cure" for his homosexuality. Regardless of the reason, his hospital stay proved to be the most pivotal moment of his life, for it was there that he met Bonnie Lou Nettles, the forty-four-year-old nurse who would become his spiritual partner and co-founder of Heaven's Gate.

Bonnie Lou Trousdale was born in Houston in 1927 and raised in a strict Baptist home. She graduated from nursing school in 1948 and married Joseph Nettles the following year, eventually having four children. As she grew older, Bonnie turned away from her Baptist roots and became deeply immersed in New Age practices. She participated in séances, believed she was clairvoyant, interpreted astrological charts with the help of a ghostly 200-year-old monk named "Brother Francis," and shared Herff's fascination with UFOs. In 1966, she joined the Houston Lodge of the Theosophical Society, an organization that encourages belief based on individual experience rather than tradition, delving deeper into esoteric beliefs. Her growing obsession with these alternative spiritualities caused a rift in her marriage. In the late 1960s, a fellow seer gave Bonnie a prophecy: in 1972, she would meet a tall, slender man with fair skin and blonde hair and when she laid eyes on Herff Applewhite in the hospital that year, she knew instantly that he was the man from the prophecy.

Bonnie approached Herff, who was in an extremely vulnerable mental state, and offered him a reading. She told him that he was a prophet sent by God, destined to guide humanity away from sin and toward the kingdom of heaven. For Herff, who felt rejected and purposeless, Bonnie's words were a lifeline. He latched onto this new identity, and the two became inseparable, their relationship described as entirely platonic. Herff moved in with the Nettles family, a bizarre situation that soon led to Bonnie and Joseph's divorce, setting them free to pursue their divine quest. They pooled their money, opened a short-lived metaphysical bookstore, and started a business teaching theosophy, a mystical belief system that tries to understand the nature of divinity and spiritual enlightenment. However, by 1973, they were broke, living out of campsites, stealing food, and dining and dashing, justifying their actions by believing they were above human laws. During this time, they consumed a wide range of literature, from religious texts to fantasy novels, and became avid watchers of *Star Trek*. Bonnie adopted Herff's short hairstyle, creating the androgynous look that would later become the cult's signature.

Their defining "epiphany" occurred in July 1973 while camping on the Oregon coast. Reading the *Book of Revelation*, they became convinced that they were the "two witnesses" described in Chapter eleven, destined to be martyred, resurrected after three and a half days, and then ascend to heaven in a cloud — which they interpreted as a UFO. This marked the birth of their core doctrine: only their most loyal followers, those who could shed their "humanness," would be allowed to transcend with them to the "Next Level" aboard the spaceship. This ascension, which they called "the demonstration," would signify the coming apocalypse. However, in August 1974, Herff was arrested for failing to return a stolen rental car and Bonnie for possessing stolen credit cards. Herff spent six months in jail.

Upon his release, the pair, now calling themselves "Bo and Peep" or simply "The Two," launched their first major recruitment effort. They traveled across the United States, posting flyers inviting people to meetings where Herff, the primary speaker, would preach their message: abandon your earthly lives, families, possessions, and desires, especially sexuality, to purify yourselves for the journey to the Next Level. They emphasized that their martyrdom and resurrection were imminent, and the spaceship could arrive any day, creating a sense of urgency. Their message resonated with a surprising number of people. In September 1975, after a single meeting in Waldport, Oregon, twenty locals vanished, leaving everything behind to join the group. People from various backgrounds, many well-educated and from comfortable families, walked away from their lives, captivated by the promise of ascension. Couples like Suzanne and Wayne Cook left their ten-year-old daughter Kelly, telling her they were going away on a spaceship and she would never see them again.

Sociologist Robert Balch, intrigued by the reports of the missing Oregonians, infiltrated the group with a colleague in 1975. They followed cryptic instructions involving a zip code book in a post office and a meeting atop Mount Diablo before being integrated into separate nomadic encampments. They spent three months living undercover within the cult. Balch noted that, at this early stage, Bo and Peep didn't employ typical coercive cult tactics; membership was voluntary, and people were free to leave at any time. Life was communal and unstructured, moving between campsites, with daily meetings where the members were given tuning forks and instructed to tune their minds to the frequency of Note A (440 Hz), though no one, including Bo and Peep, seemed to know quite what to do with them. However, when Balch published his findings, the media attention exploded and Bo and Peep's real names were revealed. The press began associating them with sinister groups like the Manson Family, even accusing them of bizarre acts like cattle mutilations. Attendance at their meetings plummeted, members started leaving, and Bo and Peep declared, "The Harvest is closed," retreating with their remaining followers into nearly two decades of seclusion.

During these years underground, the group evolved significantly. The Members stabilized at around forty core followers, mostly well-educated individuals from middle-to-upper-class backgrounds, ranging in age from sixteen to individuals in their 70s, and among them was Thomas Nichols, brother of actress Nichelle Nichols, who portrayed Uhura in *Star Trek*. They continued their nomadic existence, eventually settling into rented mansions funded by the trust fund of member David Van Sinderen, living in strict secrecy within suburban neighborhoods. It was during this period that Bo and Peep adopted their final, most enduring names: Ti

(Bonnie) and Do (Herff), inspired by Bonnie's favorite movie, *The Sound of Music*.

Life inside the "craft," as they called their homes, became highly regimented and focused on stripping away individuality. Bonnie and Herff were the "teachers" in a "classroom" designed to help members shed their human "vehicles" and prepare their alien consciousnesses for graduation to the Next Level. Any pre-existing relationships were severed, and members were assigned "check partners" for constant mutual monitoring, sometimes even accompanying each other to the bathroom. Everything was a test, and perfection was the goal.

They developed their own terminology to avoid triggering memories of their past lives: bedrooms were "rust chambers," the laundry room was a "fiber lab," bras were "slingshots," and heaven was the "Next Level." Sexual organs were referred to as "plumbing," and any sensual thought or romantic feeling was completely forbidden. Celibacy was strictly enforced, underscored by the humiliating "nocturnal emission" logbook where men had to record involuntary nighttime occurrences. Meals were strictly controlled, even pancakes had to be the exact same size. Makeup was forbidden, and everyone adopted the same short haircut and uniform-like clothing — button-up shirts, slacks, and athletic shoes — to achieve a genderless, collective identity, mirroring the Borg from *Star Trek*, a collective Herff became fascinated with. Members were given new names ending in "-ody," meaning "little member of the kingdom of heaven," further erasing their pasts. Physical abuse was absent, and members remained technically free to leave, often given bus money if they chose to depart, but the psychological control was profound and pervasive.

This secluded existence was shattered in 1985 when Bonnie was diagnosed with eye cancer. Despite surgery to remove her eye, the cancer spread rapidly to her liver, and she died on June 19, 1985, just three weeks after informing the group. Her death created a major doctrinal crisis: if they were aliens merely inhabiting human vehicles, why hadn't Bonnie simply shed her failing body and ascended? Herff quickly reformulated the narrative and explained that Ti's vehicle had simply "broken down" and that her advanced Next Level consciousness had effectively "burned up" her human form from the inside. The transformation, he now claimed, was purely spiritual; their physical bodies would be left behind on Earth. Because of cognitive dissonance (the discomfort of holding conflicting beliefs), the remaining members accepted the change, letting their need to believe outweigh the clear contradiction.

With Bonnie gone, Herff became the sole leader, assuming an even more controlling and messianic role. He declared himself Jesus Christ and Bonnie God the Father, and conducted a bizarre ceremony where he "married" every member of the group, placing a gold band on each of their fingers. However, his own struggles with his repressed sexuality continued to torment him. This culminated after Herff experienced a nocturnal emission himself, expressing intense frustration over his inability to control his urges. An enthusiastic member, Stephen McArthur (Sarody), suggested castration as a definitive solution. Herff seized upon the idea, offering it as a voluntary option to the male members. After a dangerously botched first attempt performed within the group by former nurse Julie LaMontagne (Livody), which resulted in Sarody being rushed to the hospital and his removed testicles being thrown into the ocean, they found a doctor willing to perform the procedures. Ultimately, Herff and six other men opted for castration which, due to the extremity of the action, caused some long-term members, including Wayne Cook, to leave the group, though his wife Suzanne remained.

In the early 1990s, fueled by the widespread anxiety surrounding the upcoming turn of the millennium (the "Y2K scare"), Herff decided it was time for one final recruitment effort. They launched a satellite TV series called *Beyond Human*, took out a $30,000 full-page ad in the *USA Today*, sent out VHS tapes, and even returned to holding in-person meetings. This time, however, the public was overwhelmingly skeptical and often openly hostile, mocking their beliefs and criticizing them for abandoning their families. The recruitment drive was largely a failure, attracting only a couple of new members and reinforcing Herff's belief that humanity had rejected its final chance for salvation. Influenced by the tragic events of the Waco siege in 1993 (a fifty-one-day standoff between Branch Davidians, a religious sect founded in 1955 by Benjamin Roden, and federal agents where seventy-six people died), the discussion within the group turned definitively toward planning their "exit." An initial idea to provoke a deadly confrontation with authorities was rejected by the members as too uncertain. Suicide became the agreed-upon plan, leading five members to leave the group.

The arrival of the Hale-Bopp comet in 1996 provided the final catalyst. When unfounded rumors circulated online about a massive, unidentified object four times the size of Earth trailing the comet, the members of Heaven's Gate seized upon it as the sign they had been waiting for — the spaceship carrying Bonnie had arrived to take them home to the Next Level. Though they couldn't see the non-existent object through their own high-powered telescopes, their belief was unshaken. They set their "graduation" date for March 1997, coinciding with the comet's closest approach to Earth and the Easter holiday. In their final weeks, they took celebratory trips to Sea World, Las Vegas, and Mexico. They recorded cheerful exit interviews expressing their joy at leaving their "vehicles" behind; they updated their website with a final "Red Alert" message, proclaiming Hale-Bopp as the long-awaited marker for their departure. After enjoying a last meal together at a local Marie Callender's restaurant, they methodically carried out their plan over several days starting March 22nd. They ingested a lethal cocktail of phenobarbital, a medicine used to control seizures, mixed with applesauce or pudding, washed down with vodka, and then placed plastic bags over their heads to ensure asphyxiation. They died in three staggered groups, with members of the later groups carefully cleaning and shrouding the bodies of those who had gone before. Herff himself is thought to have been in the second group. It was a calm, orderly, and deeply tragic conclusion to a twenty-two-year journey into delusion, leaving a shocked public to grapple with the incomprehensible reality of thirty-nine individuals willingly following their leader into oblivion.

The aftermath saw further tragedy, as several former members, including Wayne Cook and Chuck Humphrey, committed suicide in an attempt to "catch up" with the group they believed was now aboard the spaceship. A 1998 reunion of former members devolved into anger when letters revealed that Bonnie Nettles had secretly maintained contact with her own daughter throughout the cult's existence, a stark betrayal of the sacrifices demanded of her followers.

The story of Heaven's Gate stands as one of the most haunting examples of how faith, isolation, and psychological manipulation can intertwine to devastating effect. What began as a quest for spiritual enlightenment became a descent into delusion, driven by the insecurities and unhealed wounds of a man seeking purpose and acceptance. Through Bonnie and Herff's teachings, ordinary people were slowly reshaped into instruments of a shared fantasy, surrendering individuality, identity, and ultimately life itself in the belief that death would bring transcendence.

7

THE CARNEGIE HEIRESS

In the dazzling, often deceptive world of America's Gilded Age (a period from about the late 1870s to the late 1890s), fortunes were made, empires were built, and high society guarded its gates with fierce exclusivity. It was an era defined by staggering wealth and rigid social structures, yet it was also a time ripe for manipulation by those audacious enough to exploit the era's assumptions and vanities. Into this glittering landscape stepped a woman of humble origins and boundless nerve, a master chameleon who, through sheer force of will and a breathtaking series of lies, convinced the financial titans of her time that she was the secret, illegitimate daughter of Andrew Carnegie, then the richest man on the planet. Armed with forged documents and an uncanny ability to project an aura of immense wealth and social standing, she conned bankers and businessmen out of millions, leaving a trail of financial ruin and shattered reputations in her wake. Her name, or at least the one under which she perpetrated her most famous frauds, was Cassie L. Chadwick. Her real story, however, was a far cry from the privileged life she fabricated, a decades-long saga of deception that began long before she invoked the Carnegie name and ended behind prison walls.

Before she adopted the Chadwick persona and began weaving her elaborate Carnegie fantasy, she was Elizabeth Bigley, born in Eastwood,

Ontario, Canada, on October 10, 1857. From a young age, she reportedly displayed a "mania for fine clothing," an early indicator, perhaps, of her aspirations for a life beyond her means. Her criminal career began in early adulthood. At the age of just twenty-two, she was arrested for forgery in Woodstock, Ontario. Facing prison time, she deployed a tactic that would serve her well throughout her life: she feigned mental instability. Pleading not guilty by reason of insanity, she convinced the court of her diminished capacity and walked free.

Undeterred, Elizabeth, now operating under various aliases, set her sights on bigger targets. Three years later, in 1882, she surfaced in Cleveland, Ohio, presenting herself as a wealthy heiress. Her performance was convincing enough to capture the attention and affection of a local physician, Dr. Wallace S. Springstein. They were quickly married, but the union lasted a mere eleven days. Dr. Springstein, upon discovering his new wife's fabricated background and criminal history, promptly threw her out of his house. Her brief foray into legitimate society had ended abruptly.

Cast out but ever resourceful, the woman now known as Cassie embarked on a series of smaller, transient scams. In Erie, Pennsylvania, she adopted the name "Madame LoRuse" and cultivated friendships, hinting at vast sums of money that were temporarily inaccessible. Playing on their sympathy, she claimed to be suffering from a severe hemorrhage requiring an urgent, costly operation. To make her fictitious illness appear real, she employed a grotesque but effective trick: she would surreptitiously make her gums bleed, presenting the blood as evidence of her internal ailment. Her concerned friends, convinced of her dire situation, lent her the money she requested. She took their cash and vanished, leaving them with nothing but empty pockets and the story of her supposed affliction.

A couple of years later, now using the name "Lidley Baggley," she settled into a boarding house in another town, owned by Mrs. Hoover. By this time, Cassie was pregnant. Ever the manipulator, she wrote back to her mother and sister in Canada, claiming she had married a wealthy, elderly man named C. L. Hoover, who was conveniently deceased, and that he was the father of her child. She named her son Emil Hoover, giving him the surname of his entirely fictitious father. Motherhood, however, did not align with her ambitions. At some point, young Emil was sent to live with Cassie's mother and sister in Canada, freeing her to continue her relentless pursuit of wealth and status through deception.

Seeking a new angle, Cassie reinvented herself yet again, this time as a clairvoyant and fortune teller, operating first as "Lydia Scott" and then as the more exotic "Madame Lydia De Vere." This profession, built on illusion and suggestion, perfectly suited her talents. However, her old habits soon resurfaced. While practicing her mystical arts, she committed forgery against one of her clients, a crime that finally landed her a significant prison sentence. She was sentenced to nine and a half years in the Ohio State Penitentiary. Yet, her knack for escaping consequences persisted. After serving only four years, she was granted parole by the Governor of Ohio, William McKinley. In a strange twist of fate, just five years after granting her early release, McKinley would become the 25th President of the United States, only to be assassinated four years into his term. Cassie, meanwhile, walked out of prison, ready for her next act.

Upon her release, she once again sought the security and legitimacy of marriage to a respectable man. Working under another alias at a massage parlor, she encountered Dr. Leroy S. Chadwick, a prominent and highly respected physician in Cleveland. Whatever transpired during that initial massage appointment sparked a whirlwind romance and shortly after their meeting, in 1897, they were married. Dr. Chadwick came from a well-known and esteemed family, members of Cleveland's "400," the city's equivalent of New York's elite social register. Crucially, Dr. Chadwick knew absolutely nothing about Cassie's real family, her background, or her extensive criminal past. His relatives and friends were immediately suspicious of this mysterious woman who had appeared seemingly out of nowhere. They worried that Dr. Chadwick, known for his reserved and trusting nature, was being taken advantage of.

In the same year she married Dr. Chadwick, Cassie launched her most audacious and elaborate scheme yet. She began a fraudulent borrowing spree, securing hundreds of thousands of dollars in loans from multiple Cleveland banks. While her husband's medical practice was successful, the Chadwick name alone wouldn't qualify her for the massive sums she sought. So, she invoked a different name, one synonymous with unimaginable wealth and power: Carnegie. She boldly claimed to be the illegitimate daughter of Andrew Carnegie, the steel magnate who stood as the wealthiest man in the world at that time.

Astonishingly, the right people — people with money, bankers susceptible to the allure of prestige and connection — believed her. Her story played perfectly into the social dynamics and technological limitations of the era. Illegitimacy, particularly among the wealthy, was a scandalous but not uncommon secret, something whispered about but rarely confirmed. Cassie's willingness to confide this sensitive detail lent her story an air of authenticity, and thanks to the rudimentary identification systems, as there were no driver's licenses or sophisticated databases to verify her claims, she got away with it. After all, who would dare to question Andrew Carnegie directly about such a delicate personal matter?

Cassie played her part flawlessly. She dressed in the finest clothes, displayed impeccable manners, and moved through society with the practiced ease of inherited wealth. She presented herself as Carnegie's cherished but secret daughter, well-provided for by a father who felt a sense of obligation, even if he couldn't publicly acknowledge her. To back up her claims, she produced forged documents: promissory notes and securities certificates purportedly signed by Carnegie himself, promising repayment and listing collateral supposedly worth millions. She even fabricated evidence of a trust fund established for her, valued at over $10 million (about $350 million today). Faced with these seemingly legitimate documents bearing the signature of the world's richest man, and charmed by Cassie's convincing portrayal of a discreetly cared-for heiress, the bankers readily opened their vaults.

Her audacity grew with each successful loan. She secured large sums from prominent Cleveland institutions like the Euclid Avenue Savings and Trust, which gave her $382,000 (about $13 million today) and the American Exchange National Bank, which gave her $8,800 (about $313,000 today), as well as smaller banks like the Wade Park Banking Company, which gave her $40,000 (about $1.4 million today) and the Savings Deposit Bank of Elyria, which gave her $10,000 (about $350,000 today). But her most significant victim was Charles Beckwith, the president of the tiny Citizens National Bank in Oberlin, Ohio. By the time Cassie encountered him, her confidence was absolute. She wasn't asking for tens of thousands; she requested a staggering $340,000 (about $12 million today), including $100,000 (about $3.5 million today) as a personal loan. Beckwith, reportedly smitten with her, and reassured by the forged Carnegie notes, gave her everything she asked for. This single act of reckless lending, based entirely on Cassie's lies, would ultimately bankrupt his small bank. Altogether, Cassie Chadwick managed to steal an estimated $2 million (about $70 million today) by jumping between cities in Ohio, Massachusetts, and New York, all while claiming to be Andrew Carnegie's secret love child.

Her extravagant charade finally began to unravel in 1904. A Massachusetts man named Herbert B. Newton, a broker she had duped, filed a lawsuit against her, claiming she had stolen $190,800 (about $7 million today) from him using the same forged Carnegie notes as security. Newton's public accusation acted like a dam breaking; suddenly, other bankers and businessmen who had been quietly trying to recover their losses, perhaps too embarrassed to admit they had been swindled, came forward with their own lawsuits. The cumulative claims quickly reached over a quarter of a million dollars, and that only accounted for those willing to publicly admit their folly.

With her web of deceit collapsing, Cassie fled, but the law caught up with her on December 2, 1904. Police tracked her down to a room at the Hotel Breslin in Manhattan, apparently preparing to flee the state or even the country. When they arrested her, they discovered $100,000 (about $3.5 million today) in cash strapped around her waist. Her time playing the role of an elite socialite was over.

Cassie's trial was a sensation, laying bare the full scope of her decades-long criminal career. Details of her previous aliases, frauds, the faked hemorrhage, the fabricated wealthy husband, the fortune-telling scams, her earlier prison sentence, and even a faked death notice she sent to friends in 1883 were all brought to light. The sheer audacity and longevity of her deception shocked the public. Her estranged husband, Dr. Chadwick, who had moved to Europe with his daughter, was initially charged alongside her, under the assumption that he must have been complicit. However, he sailed back to the United States for the trial and was quickly exonerated, proving he had been as clueless as everyone else about his wife's elaborate deceptions.

Despite the overwhelming evidence against her, Cassie maintained an air of detachment throughout the proceedings. Due to hearing loss she had developed, she didn't even hear the clerk read the guilty verdict on seven counts of conspiracy. When her attorney finally leaned in and told her, "We have lost, Mrs. Chadwick," the color drained from her face. She sank into her chair, and as she was led away to her jail cell, she cried out, "Let me go! Oh my God, let me go! I'm not guilty! I'm not guilty, I tell you! Let me go!" before fainting.

Her sentencing hearing drew considerable attention, notably attended by Andrew Carnegie himself, the man whose name she had so brazenly exploited. She was sentenced to fourteen years in prison and fined $70,000 (about $2.5 million today) — a paltry sum compared to the millions she had stolen. The true cost of her crimes was borne not just by the banks, but by their everyday account holders. This was before the establishment of the Federal Deposit Insurance Corporation (FDIC) in 1933; when a bank failed due to fraud like Cassie's, depositors lost everything.

One group of victims was Oberlin College, which had deposited its funds in Charles Beckwith's now-closed Citizens National Bank. At the sentencing hearing, when it was revealed that Cassie's fraud had cost the college $50,000 (about $1.7 million today), Andrew Carnegie stepped in — whether out of responsibility or his usual philanthropy — to cover the loss. He replaced the lost funds and donated an additional $100,000 (about $3.5 million today) for the construction of a new library on campus, a building that still stands today. Carnegie reportedly felt horrible for the victims and assisted others as well.

The most tragic figure in the aftermath was Charles Beckwith. Financially ruined, his bank shuttered, and having served jail time himself for his reckless mismanagement of depositors' funds, he remained inexplicably loyal to Cassie. He visited her in prison, telling her, "I am not convinced that you are a fraud, and I look for the time when everything will be straightened out." He pleaded with her to make a statement that could clear his name, but she refused, reportedly laughing in his face. Just weeks after that prison visit, Beckwith died in shame — blind, paralyzed, and delirious, using his last breaths to speak of Cassie. When news of his death reached Cassie in her cell, she initially feigned indifference to the press but later confided to a cellmate that the news left her "pained beyond expression."

Cassie Chadwick began serving her sentence on January 12, 1906, and on October 10, 1907, on her fiftieth birthday, she died. The prison doctor attributed her death to a "bad heart," a diagnosis few who knew her story would have disputed. The woman who had charmed, manipulated, and swindled her way through life, leaving a trail of broken banks and broken men, had finally run out of time and illusions.

8

THE BOY WHO BURNED
DOWN THE LAW

It was a sweltering summer night in Lawrence County, Alabama, the kind where the heat clings heavy and damp, refusing to yield even after the sun dips below the horizon. In the small, rural community, the air hung thick with the sounds of cicadas and the distant bark of dogs. But the oppressive stillness of that July night in 2003 was about to be shattered by an act of shocking brutality, forever altering the lives of everyone involved and igniting a legal firestorm that would eventually reach the highest court in the United States. At the center of this maelstrom was a skinny, unassuming fourteen-year-old boy named Evan James Miller, a child whose broken past and momentary, monstrous actions would inadvertently place him at the forefront of a landmark battle over juvenile justice in America.

Evan Miller's young life had been a chaotic shuffle through poverty, neglect, and violence. Bouncing between foster care placements and a home environment saturated with abuse and instability, he carried the visible and invisible scars of a deeply troubled childhood. His mother struggled, and his father's presence was marked more by harm than help. Evan had attempted suicide multiple times, cycled through psychological programs, and developed a dependency on drugs — all before he was old enough to legally drive a car. He was a child adrift, shaped by chaos and trauma, lacking the guidance and stability necessary to navigate the treacherous path to adulthood.

On the night of July 15, 2003, Evan was spending time with a slightly older friend, sixteen-year-old Colby Smith. They ended up at the nearby mobile home of a neighbor, fifty-two-year-old Cole C. Cannon. Cannon had only recently moved into the Country Living trailer park, occupying the trailer just in front of where Evan lived with his mother. According to later testimony, Cannon appeared to have been drinking heavily that evening; Colby Smith recalled that he smelled of alcohol and was staggering. He had come over to the Millers' trailer earlier, complaining he'd burned his dinner and asking for something to eat. While Evan's mother, Susan, prepared some spaghetti for Cannon, Evan and Colby slipped over to Cannon's trailer. Their initial intent, according to Smith, was to look for drugs, but they found none. Instead, they stumbled upon Cole Cannon's baseball card collection — a remnant from years prior when he owned a card shop — and pocketed some of the cards, hiding them away before returning to Evan's trailer.

When Cannon finished eating and went back to his own trailer, Evan and Colby followed him a short time later. Their plan, Smith testified, was now to get Cannon drunk and steal his money. They shared marijuana with him, smoked a joint, and played drinking games until Cannon, heavily intoxicated, eventually passed out on his couch. While Cannon was unconscious, Evan found his wallet, took it into the bathroom, and removed the cash inside, a little over $300, which he then split with Colby. The theft should have been the end of it, a petty crime committed by two troubled teenagers against an incapacitated man. But the situation took a sudden, violent turn.

As Evan attempted to slide the now-empty wallet back into Cannon's pocket, the older man abruptly woke up and lunged, grabbing Evan by the throat. Colby Smith, witnessing the altercation, reacted instantly. He grabbed a nearby baseball bat and struck Cannon hard on the head. The blow stunned Cannon, releasing his grip on Evan. But the violence didn't stop there. Evan, now free, climbed onto Cannon and began pummeling him furiously with his fists. Cannon pleaded with them to stop, but his cries went unheeded. Evan picked up the baseball bat that Colby had dropped and continued the assault, striking Cannon repeatedly with brutal force. The beating was merciless, fueled perhaps by Evan's own history as a victim of abuse, now tragically transformed into a perpetrator. At some point during the assault, Evan reportedly placed a sheet or shirt over Cannon's battered head and uttered chilling words: "Cole, I am God. I come to take your life."

After Evan delivered a final blow with the bat, he and Colby fled back to the Miller trailer, leaving Cannon broken and bleeding on the floor. But within minutes, they returned, perhaps realizing the gravity of what they had done or simply trying to cover their tracks. They made a cursory attempt to clean up the blood that was splattered on the walls and furniture. Then, their thoughts turned to destroying the evidence entirely. They decided to set the trailer on fire. Colby used a lighter to ignite a couch in the back bedroom, while Evan started another fire on a different couch. As they were leaving the rapidly burning trailer, Colby saw Cannon still lying helplessly on the floor. In a fleeting moment of what he later described as pity, Colby placed a towel under Cannon's head in a futile attempt to stanch the bleeding and turned on the kitchen faucet, stopping up the sink in a desperate, illogical hope that the water might extinguish the flames. As they finally exited the burning trailer, they heard Cole Cannon's faint, haunting question drift through the smoke: "Why are y'all doing this to me?" About ten minutes later, Colby returned to the trailer alone, perhaps driven by guilt or morbid curiosity. He could hear Cannon coughing inside, but smoke was pouring out, and he saw Evan approaching, so he turned and fled back to the Miller residence for good. Cole Cannon was left to die in the inferno.

Firefighters from the Speake Volunteer Fire Department responded to the blaze in the early morning hours of July 16th. While extinguishing the fire, they noticed blood spatter on a wall and blood saturating a coffee table, immediately indicating that this was more than a simple house fire. Their search led them to the discovery of Cole Cannon's body in the hallway. The fire marshal, Richard Montgomery, conducted the initial investigation and quickly determined the fire was suspicious, noting multiple points of origin, and turned the case over to Investigator Tim Sandlin of the Lawrence County Sheriff's Department.

Investigator Sandlin began piecing together the events. After speaking with Cannon's family, he learned that certain items were missing from the trailer, including his wallet and some baseball trading cards. The wallet was later found stuffed under the couch, but Cannon's driver's license was gone. Sandlin also recovered the baseball bat from beneath the couch. These findings led him directly to the neighboring trailer occupied by Evan Miller and his mother, Susan. Susan Miller voluntarily gave Investigator Sandlin a box of trading cards, and both she and Evan agreed to accompany him to the sheriff's office to provide statements.

At the station, Evan was read his rights from a juvenile Miranda form, which both he and his mother signed. Initially, Evan stuck to a simple story: he had been home watching a movie, admitted Cannon had visited their trailer earlier, but denied ever going over to Cannon's trailer himself. He claimed he only learned about the fire when the fire department arrived the next morning. However, as Investigator Sandlin pressed him, asking him to recount the events backward from the morning, Evan became agitated. "Forget all that," he snapped, "that wasn't true." He then requested that everyone except Investigator Sandlin leave the room. With his mother and juvenile officers gone, Evan provided a second statement. He admitted going to Cannon's trailer, finding the trading cards, and returning later with Colby to drink beer. He described Cannon becoming heavily intoxicated and falling, then claimed Cannon grabbed him by the throat when he tried to help. He stated that Colby pushed Cannon off him, Cannon grabbed the bat, hit Evan with it, Colby then took the bat and hit Cannon, before Evan kicked the bat under the couch. He admitted to punching Cannon several times and finding the wallet on the floor, taking the cash and the driver's license. He ended his account by claiming he and Colby ran out the back door when they heard his mother knocking, warning that the police were coming, and heard Cannon ask why they did it as they fled. Significantly, this second statement made no mention of the brutal beating with the bat after the initial altercation, nor did it include any admission of setting the fires.

Evan's partial admission, however, was enough to prompt a full fire investigation at Cannon's trailer on July 24th. Deputy Fire Marshal Bo Lynden Blackton confirmed the extensive blood spatter and identified four separate points of origin for the fire, clearly indicating arson.

Meanwhile, the initial external examination of Cannon's body by forensic pathologist Dr. Adam Craig had yielded a perplexing result. Seeing no obvious signs of foul play beyond what could be attributed to the fire, Dr. Craig initially ruled the death an accident caused by smoke and soot inhalation and did not perform a full autopsy. However, based on the developing evidence from the investigation, Investigator Sandlin requested that Cannon's body be exhumed for a more thorough examination. On August 1st, 2003, Dr. Craig performed the full autopsy. He discovered significant injuries hidden beneath the fire damage: a two-inch (about five centimeters) contusion on the forehead caused by blunt force, and six rib fractures on both sides of the body. Hemorrhaging confirmed these injuries occurred before Cannon died. Dr. Craig revised his findings, reaffirming smoke inhalation as the primary cause of death but adding multiple blunt force injuries and ethanol intoxication as significant contributing factors that likely prevented Cannon from escaping the burning trailer.

While the forensic evidence mounted, Evan Miller made further incriminating statements, seemingly unprompted. During transport to mental health evaluations on July 31st and August 4th, he spoke with Deputy Tim McWhorter. Though not interrogated, Evan initiated conversations about the case. He asked the deputy if he would get in trouble for changing his story to tell the truth, admitted he was "not innocent" and had been involved in the assault, and stated he deserved to serve time. He claimed he had been "really messed up" on Klonopin and whiskey that night. He repeated the story of Cannon grabbing him by the neck but added that he then "slammed Mr. Cannon really hard" because he was "really pissed off," and admitted they had "roughed him up pretty good," acknowledging the autopsy would show bruises. He claimed memory lapses but conceded, the more he thought about it, the more it made him think he started the fire.

DNA analysis provided further corroboration. Nancy Jones, head of the DNA section at the state forensic lab, testified that blood found on a cushion and the wall matched Cole Cannon's DNA profile. Bloodstains consistent with Evan Miller's DNA were found on two T-shirts recovered from the scene; one of these shirts also possibly contained Cannon's blood, and the spatter patterns were consistent with impact from an object, not a gunshot. While usable DNA could not be obtained from the bat itself or the towel placed under Cannon's head, the collective evidence painted a damning picture.

Evan Miller, now seventeen years old, after lengthy juvenile proceedings and certification as an adult, finally went on trial for capital murder in October 2006. His defense claimed he was not guilty due to mental illness, with his mother and a psychologist testifying about his troubled past — suicide attempts, time in foster care, drug use, and diagnoses such as conduct disorder, personality disorder, depression, and oppositional defiant disorder. His accomplice, Colby Smith, had accepted a plea deal the previous week, pleading guilty to felony murder in exchange for a life sentence with the possibility of parole, contingent on his testimony against Evan. The prosecution presented the forensic evidence, Smith's testimony, and Evan's own incriminating statements.

On October 20th, 2006, the Lawrence County jury returned their verdict. After initially returning confused, having found Evan guilty of everything including lesser charges, they were reinstructed and sent back. They ultimately found Evan Miller guilty of capital murder committed during the course of first-degree arson. Under Alabama law at the time, this conviction carried a mandatory sentence: life in prison without the possibility of parole. Circuit Judge Philip Reich imposed the sentence immediately. Before being led away, Evan offered a muffled apology to Cannon's family. Candy Cheatham, Cannon's oldest daughter, responded with a raw and powerful victim impact statement, showing Evan pictures of her father as a child that she had salvaged from the ashes. "You say you're sorry," she said, her voice thick with grief and anger. "You have no idea what kind of pain we went through... He was a person and he mattered to us. I do hope when you're in prison, you will find Jesus. But I can't forgive you right now. And I don't think my family can either." Evan's own family wept, his sister Aubrey later telling reporters that while her brother deserved punishment, he shouldn't have been tried as an adult and that their parents shared the blame for the neglect and abuse that shaped him.

The mandatory life-without-parole sentence imposed on a seventeen-year-old for a crime committed at fourteen placed Evan Miller's case at the center of a burgeoning legal challenge to juvenile sentencing practices. Advocacy groups, notably the Equal Justice Initiative (EJI), took up his cause, arguing that sentencing children to die in prison violated the Eighth Amendment's prohibition against cruel and unusual punishment. The case eventually made its way to the United States Supreme Court. Candy Cheatham expressed frustration with how the EJI presented the facts of the case in their briefs, feeling they downplayed Evan's culpability and unfairly maligned her father's character.

In June 2012, the Supreme Court delivered its landmark ruling in *Miller v. Alabama*. The Court held that mandatory life-without-parole sentences for individuals under the age of eighteen at the time of their crimes are unconstitutional. The ruling did not ban life-without-parole sentences for juveniles outright, but it required that sentencing judges consider the unique circumstances of the child offender — their age, maturity level, background, and the nature of the crime — before imposing such a severe sentence. The decision fundamentally reshaped juvenile justice, affirming the principle that "children are different" and possess a greater capacity for change and rehabilitation than adults. For Evan Miller, the ruling meant his mandatory sentence was vacated, and he was entitled to a new sentencing hearing where his youth and background could be properly considered. Eventually, he received his new sentencing hearing in Alabama and, in March 2017, Evan Miller was re-sentenced to life with the possibility of parole after serving thirty years. His story, which began with a brutal act in a small Alabama town, had inadvertently led to a profound shift in American law, forcing the justice system to confront the complex question of whether a child, no matter how heinous their crime, can ever truly be beyond redemption.

9

THE MAN WITHOUT A NAME

On the morning of June 16, 2009, a father and his son went for an early morning swim at Rosses Point, a scenic beach in County Sligo, Ireland. The Irish coast, even in June, can be brisk and bracing, a place of rugged beauty where the Atlantic meets the shore with a steady, rhythmic pulse. As they made their way along the sand, they saw a figure washed up at the water's edge. It was the body of a middle-aged man, and it was immediately clear that he was dead. By 8:10 a.m., he was officially pronounced dead at the scene, and his body was transported to the morgue at Sligo University Hospital for an autopsy. There was no identification found on or near him, no wallet, no phone, nothing to give a name to the face of the man who had met his end on that quiet beach. He was a ghost, a John Doe whose final moments were a complete mystery. Later, he would be buried in an unmarked grave in Sligo, his funeral attended only by police officers who had been tasked with the impossible job of figuring out who he was.

Thanks to CCTV, investigators were able to piece together the man's last few days with remarkable clarity. But the copious amounts of video evidence they uncovered did not solve the mystery; instead, they deepened it, revealing a man who moved through the world with a singular, chilling purpose: to systematically erase himself from existence. Who was this man, how did he manage to leave no trace of his life behind, and what was the significance of the mysterious purple plastic bag he was seen carrying all over town? The case that unfolded was a modern-day echo of the famous Tamám Shud mystery, a perplexing tale of a man who seemed to materialize out of thin air only to vanish into the great unknown, leaving behind a trail of carefully curated questions.

The first confirmed sighting of the mystery man was on Friday, June 12, 2009, when he arrived in the city of Derry by bus. From there, he immediately caught another bus to Sligo, a popular coastal town in the northwest of Ireland. Upon his arrival, he hailed a taxi and asked the driver to take him to a cheap hotel. The first option was fully booked, so the driver took him to his next suggestion, the Sligo City Hotel. Hotel security cameras captured his entrance. He was a man of medium build, dressed neatly in dark trousers, a shirt, and a leather jacket, carrying a black shoulder bag and another larger black bag in his hand. He approached the front desk, paid cash in advance for a three-night stay, and gave his name as Peter Bergmann. In the hotel register, he wrote down an address: Ainstettersnstrasse 15, Vienna, 4472, Austria. Both the taxi driver and the hotel staff noted that he spoke with a thick German or Austrian accent. In what would later become a critical point of frustration for investigators, the hotel, apparently against its own policy, did not ask him for any form of identification. Peter Bergmann, a man with no verifiable past, had officially checked in.

The next day, Saturday, June 13th, the man began a strange and methodical ritual. He was captured on CCTV coming and going from the hotel a total of thirteen times. Each time he left, he was carrying a full purple plastic bag. The contents were impossible to see on the grainy footage, but the bag was clearly weighted with objects. And each time he returned to the hotel, the purple bag was gone. He was also seen visiting the local post office that Saturday, where he purchased eight stamps for overseas postage and a corresponding number of airmail stickers. Sligo has an extensive network of surveillance cameras covering its town center, and Bergmann was visible on many of them as he walked the streets. But in all that footage, he was never once caught in the act of disposing of the contents of the purple bag. What he was getting rid of and where he was leaving it remains a complete mystery.

The following day, Sunday, June 14th, Bergmann's activities took a different turn. He hailed another taxi and asked the driver to recommend a quiet, secluded beach where he might go for a swim. The driver took him to Rosses Point, about five miles (about eight kilometers) out of town. Bergmann got out of the cab, took a brief look around the beach, and then, without explanation, got right back in and asked to be driven back to Sligo. It was a reconnaissance mission. The driver later confirmed that during their conversation, Bergmann mentioned he was from Austria, reinforcing the identity he had constructed at the hotel. His use of taxis seemed at odds with his choice of a cheap hotel, a small detail that suggested he was not without funds but was perhaps being careful and deliberate in his choices.

Monday, June 15th, was Peter Bergmann's last full day of life. He requested a late checkout from the hotel and then went out one last time, again carrying the full purple plastic bag for its final emptying. When he checked out of the hotel later that day, the CCTV footage showed him with his black shoulder bag and the purple plastic bag, but the larger black bag he had arrived with was now gone. In its place was a much smaller bag, something that looked more like a wash bag. He walked to the bus station, and by the time he appeared on the cameras there, this smaller black bag had also disappeared. Inside the station, he ordered a cappuccino and a toasted cheese and ham sandwich, a classic meal for someone waiting to travel. He then took a piece of paper from his pocket, wrote some notes on it, folded it up, and then meticulously tore it into tiny pieces, scattering the confetti remains into a nearby public bin. Finally, he boarded the bus for Rosses Point, the beach he had scouted out the day before. When the driver asked if he wanted a single or a return ticket, he asked for a single.

The bus arrived at Rosses Point in the mid-afternoon, and Bergmann disembarked, carrying what little he had left. Several people confirmed seeing him on the beach over the course of that afternoon and evening. He stood out. Most witnesses remembered him being quite smartly dressed for a day at the beach, wearing his dark trousers, shirt, and leather jacket. One witness later said that he looked "almost out of place and out of time." He was seen walking parallel to the water's edge with his trousers rolled up, pacing up and down the sand with his hands clasped behind his back, as if he were "in another world." He responded to brief greetings from fellow beachgoers but otherwise kept to himself. The last confirmed sighting of him alive was after 10:30 p.m., with some sources placing it as late as 11:50 p.m. It was only the fact that he was there so late that made anyone remember seeing him at all. The next morning, his lifeless body was found washed up on the sand. He was wearing Speedo-style swimming trunks, but strangely, he had his underwear and a T-shirt over them. His other clothes, including his leather jacket, were found in a neatly folded pile further up the beach. There was no form of ID on his body, only a few coins and some minor personal items. And just like his other belongings, every single tag had been cut from his clothing.

The initial assumption was that he had drowned, a logical conclusion for a man found washed up on a beach in swimming gear. But the autopsy revealed a far more complex picture. The medical examiner confirmed there were no signs of foul play, but also, crucially, no evidence of saltwater drowning. Further examination revealed that Bergmann was a very sick man. He had advanced prostate cancer, with tumors that had metastasized into his bones and other organs. He had also suffered from at least two previous heart attacks. Yet, the toxicology report came back with no trace of any painkillers in his system, something the examiner found highly unusual for someone who must have been in a considerable amount of pain. Given the advanced stage of his cancer, it was likely he had only weeks, if not days, to live. The official cause of death was listed as acute cardiac arrest. He had intended to go into the sea, but it seemed his own failing heart had claimed him before the water could.

The name Peter Bergmann and the Austrian address were quickly found to be fictitious. Searches of European, North American, and South American passport databases yielded no matches. Stills from the CCTV footage and an artist's rendering based on his autopsy photos were circulated throughout Ireland and Europe, but no family member, no friend, no former colleague ever came forward to identify the man. None of his bags or any of the items he had so carefully disposed of around Sligo were ever found. It was as if Peter Bergmann was a ghost who had walked the earth for a few days and then simply dissolved.

Everything about his behavior pointed to a man who had come to Sligo with the sole intention of ending his life and leaving no trace of his existence behind. But why go to such extraordinary lengths to ensure his anonymity? One theory revolved around insurance. In some countries, life insurance policies are voided in the event of a suicide. By making it seem as though he had simply disappeared, he could eventually be declared legally dead, allowing a potential payout for his family. This theory, however, has a significant flaw: he seemed to have no dependents or anyone he wished to notify of his death, so who would the insurance policy benefit?

A more plausible, and far more depressing, theory centers on the contents of the purple plastic bag. The sheer number of trips he made — at least thirteen — suggested he was disposing of more than just a few changes of clothes. One of the most poignant theories is that he was getting rid of items related to his illness that he found embarrassing, such as adult diapers, a common necessity for those with advanced prostate cancer. He may not have wanted the hotel staff to see them in his room's bin, and so he took it upon himself to dispose of them discreetly in public trash cans around the town. The police did search public areas, but without knowing what they were looking for, such items would have been easily overlooked. His apparent knowledge of the CCTV camera locations, which some have suggested points to spy training, is more likely the common sense of a man who was simply observant. The cameras in Sligo are highly visible, and it would not take a trained operative to notice where they were and, more importantly, where they were not.

The letters he mailed from the post office add another layer to the mystery. Were they final farewells to loved ones, explaining his decision and asking them to respect his wish for anonymity? If so, it would explain why no one ever came forward. It's a sad thought, a man so alone at the end that his final resting place is an unmarked, shared grave, his funeral attended only by strangers. It's also possible that his family and friends simply never saw the media appeals, which were largely confined to Ireland and parts of Europe.

Every potential clue seemed to lead to another dead end. While the labels on his clothes were cut off, the brands were still identifiable: his shoes were

German-made, and his jacket and trousers were from C&A, a Dutch store popular across Europe. The items in his pockets — plasters from the German brand Hansaplast, German-distributed aspirin, and a generic bar of hotel soap not available in Ireland — all pointed to a European, likely German-speaking, origin. But these items are so widely available that they provided no concrete leads. His fingerprints and DNA were taken, but they matched no one in any criminal database. In a move that has frustrated online sleuths for years, the Gardaí have officially stated that they will not submit his DNA to commercial ancestry sites, citing privacy concerns.

In the end, the most probable conclusion is also the simplest and the most tragic. Peter Bergmann was likely a quiet, lonely man, ravaged by a terminal illness and in immense, unmedicated pain, who decided to take control of his own end. He traveled to a place he had perhaps visited before, or maybe just picked from a map, and spent his final days meticulously erasing his past to spare anyone the burden of his death. The letters he posted were his true goodbyes, sent to the few people who mattered, asking them to respect his final wish. The heart attack may have been unplanned, a sudden end to a journey that was meant to conclude in the cold embrace of the Atlantic, but the end result was the same. In an age of total surveillance, digital footprints, and international communication, the man known as Peter Bergmann achieved something remarkable: he gave himself a new name, and then he disappeared, leaving behind only the ghost of a story and the enduring question of whether we should even be trying to find him at all.

$$10$$

THE NATIONAL FOREST KILLER

In the quiet woods of Cherokee County, Georgia, a sheriff's deputy noticed a white van parked conspicuously on private hunting lands. Assuming it was likely a simple case of trespassing, he approached the vehicle, where an older man with a scruffy beard was arranging maps. The man explained he was just preparing to camp briefly before moving on, chatting amiably about the strictness of the landowners and even joking lightly about hunters mistaking his colorful gear for game. Beneath this friendly, almost folksy demeanor, however, lurked a calculating predator, a man whose recent past was marked by murder and whose mind concealed far darker intentions. When the deputy requested identification, the man retrieved a fanny pack and assured him there were no weapons, casually pointing out an expandable police baton in the van as he did so. Finding no outstanding warrants or immediate cause for concern, the deputy allowed Gary Michael Hilton to leave, unaware that he had just released a dangerous killer back into the wild.

The first sign that something was terribly wrong emerged further south, in Leon County, Florida. On Sunday, December 2, 2007, forty-six-year-old Cheryl Dunlap, a dedicated nurse at Florida State University and a devout Christian active in her church, failed to show up for her Sunday school class. Concern grew the following day when she missed work, an uncharacteristic absence that prompted a friend to report her missing. Her adult son went to her home, hoping for a simple explanation, but found only her beloved dog, alone and unsettled. Police soon determined that no one had heard from Cheryl since the morning of Saturday, December 1st, when she told a friend she was heading to the library. Records confirmed she had logged onto a computer at the Wakulla County Public Library at 9:45 a.m. and cashed a check for $100 at a bank around 11:15 a.m. After that, she vanished.

Friends initially considered the possibility that Cheryl, who had recently expressed a desire for more adventure in her life, might have simply decided to leave town abruptly. But that scenario seemed increasingly unlikely given her strong ties to her community, her job, her sons, and her deep faith. Any hope for an innocent explanation evaporated that afternoon when Cheryl's car was discovered abandoned off a road near Leon Sinks Geological State Park, a popular area for hiking. There was no sign of Cheryl. Her purse and keys were still inside the vehicle, her belongings scattered across the seat, and ominously, one of the rear tires was flat. A closer examination revealed the tire hadn't just gone flat; it appeared to have been deliberately punctured. Signs of foul play were mounting, sending waves of fear and turmoil through her circle of friends and family. Her son recalled his last, brief phone conversation with her weeks earlier, a missed connection that now felt like a haunting regret.

Cheryl Dunlap's picture was quickly disseminated through local media. A couple came forward, reporting they had seen her at Leon Sinks on the afternoon of December 1st, sitting peacefully on a bench, reading a book. This placed her at the park but offered no clue as to what happened next. The investigation took a sinister turn when police checked her bank records. Cheryl's ATM card had been used five times between December 2nd and December 4th, withdrawing a total of over $700. Her family knew Cheryl would never have willingly given up her PIN. Investigators rushed to the bank, hoping surveillance footage might reveal who was accessing her account, finding their worst fears confirmed. The grainy ATM video showed not Cheryl, but a tall, thin figure, their face obscured by a disturbing, crudely made mask, methodically withdrawing cash from her account. The identity of the person behind the mask was a complete mystery, leaving Cheryl's loved ones grappling with dread and helplessness.

A month later, the nightmare seemed to repeat itself, this time over 300 miles (about 480 kilometers) north in the mountains of Georgia. On January 1st, 2008, twenty-four-year-old Meredith Emerson, an avid hiker, left a note for her roommate saying she was taking her black Labrador retriever, Ella, for a hike on Blood Mountain, one of her favorite spots along the Appalachian Trail. When she failed to return by the next morning, her roommate reported her missing. Meredith's boyfriend found her car parked at one of the trailheads, covered in snow. A frantic search began, involving friends, police, the Georgia Bureau of Investigation (GBI), and eventually, scores of volunteers.

As news of her disappearance spread, investigators spoke to several people who had been hiking on Blood Mountain on New Year's Day. They recalled seeing Meredith and Ella, but they also noticed something else: an older man lurking nearby. One witness described coming across a disturbed section of the trail shortly after seeing Meredith and the man, suggesting a struggle had taken place. Left behind on the ground were several items: Meredith's water bottles, Ella's leash, and, most ominously, an expandable police baton. Witnesses provided a consistent description of the man: white, around sixty years old, roughly 5'10" (about 177 centimeters) and 160 pounds (about seventy kilograms), with graying hair. They also mentioned another crucial detail: he had a large, reddish-colored dog with him.

Police shared these details, and tips began pouring in. Could this man be responsible for Meredith's disappearance? Could he even be the same sinister figure in the mask who had drained Cheryl Dunlap's bank account just a month earlier? The parallels were chilling: two women, alone in national forest areas, both now missing under suspicious circumstances.

Back in Leon County, Florida, the investigation into Cheryl's disappearance was also receiving tips that took on a disturbingly familiar shape. Multiple witnesses independently reported encountering a specific man in the Leon Sinks area in late November 2007, just days before Cheryl vanished. Their descriptions matched the man seen on Blood Mountain: older, skinny, scruffy, sometimes described as homeless-looking, often accompanied by a large reddish dog, variously identified as an Irish Setter or a dark Golden Retriever. Several witnesses noted feeling unnerved by him; one mentioned a long knife strapped to his side, another simply said, "He gave me the creeps." One hiker, disturbed by the encounter, had even joked grimly to her companion, "Man, that guy's killed like ten people." An older man, a white van (mentioned by some Florida witnesses), a red dog — the details were strikingly consistent across both states.

The critical break came when a Georgia businessman named John Taber heard the description of the man sought in connection with Meredith Emerson's disappearance. He immediately called the GBI tip line. Taber explained that the man they were looking for had worked for him intermittently for years, selling house siding, right up until he had recently demanded money and threatened to kill Taber. He confirmed the man drove a white Chevrolet Astro van and had a reddish Golden Retriever named Dandy. His name, Taber told the stunned investigators, was Gary Michael Hilton.

Armed with a name and driver's license photo, the GBI issued an updated "Be On the Lookout" alert. Gary Michael Hilton was officially named a person of interest in Meredith Emerson's disappearance. The race to find him intensified, fueled by the desperate hope that Meredith might still be alive.

Tragically, in Florida, that hope had already been extinguished. On December 15, 2007, two weeks after Cheryl Dunlap was last seen, a hunter walking his dogs deep in the Apalachicola National Forest stumbled upon a gruesome scene. Buzzards circling overhead led him to what appeared, at first glance, like animal remains partially covered by tree limbs and palmetto fronds. But as he got closer, he realized the horrifying truth: it was a human body, nude and significantly decomposed. The body had been horrifically mutilated. The hands and head were missing, and the nipples had been cut off. Due to the advanced decomposition and decapitation, the medical examiner could only determine the cause of death as "undetermined homicidal violence." Later, by comparing a DNA profile generated from a thigh muscle sample to known records, it was determined that the body belonged to Cheryl Dunlap.

The search for Hilton in Georgia reached a critical point on January 4th, three days after Meredith vanished. Ella, Meredith's black lab, was spotted wandering into a Kroger supermarket in Cumming, Georgia, nearly fifty miles (about eighty kilometers) south of Blood Mountain. Her microchip confirmed her identity. While Meredith's family was relieved Ella was safe, her discovery so far from the mountain, without Meredith, was deeply concerning. Later that same day, police received another crucial tip: a woman reported that Gary Hilton had called her demanding money. The call was traced to a payphone at a QuikTrip gas station, located directly across the street from the Kroger where Ella had been found. Investigators rushed to the scene, but Hilton was gone. However, in the dumpster behind the gas station, they made a grim discovery: bloody clothing, Meredith's purse, and her wallet containing her driver's license and student ID cards. The hunt for Gary Hilton had become a desperate race against time.

That night, the 911 calls police had been waiting for finally came in. Multiple callers reported seeing a man matching Hilton's description, along with his distinctive white van and red dog, at a Chevron gas station in nearby Chamblee. Witnesses described him acting suspiciously, pulling items out of his van and throwing them into the dumpster. "He's going to be gone if somebody doesn't get here," one caller urged. Police converged on the location. As officers arrived, Hilton went flat on the ground and was taken into custody without a struggle. His van and his dog, Dandy, were secured. But the relief of his capture was immediately tempered by a stark, unsettling reality: Meredith Emerson was nowhere to be found.

Hilton was transported to GBI headquarters, where he initially proved utterly uncooperative, lying prone on the floor, refusing to answer questions, and complaining of pain from multiple sclerosis. Investigators noted fresh scratches on his face and neck, along with a badly swollen right hand — possible defensive wounds. With Meredith's fate hanging in the balance, they needed Hilton to talk. Agent Clay Bridges appealed to his conscience, "You need to go ahead and just tell us where she's at." But Hilton remained silent.

While Hilton stonewalled, evidence continued to mount. Investigators processing his van found blood that matched Meredith's DNA. Meanwhile, in Florida, police searching campsites near where Hilton had been seen around the time of Cheryl Dunlap's disappearance made a horrifying discovery: a burn pit containing charred human finger bones and skull fragments. DNA identification was impossible due to the condition of the remains, but authorities were almost certain they belonged to Cheryl. At one of these campsites, investigators also found zip ties, matching the description of those potentially used on Meredith, and crucially, a cigarette butt containing Hilton's DNA. Further solidifying the link between the two cases, forensic analysis confirmed that the bayonet-style knife recovered from the struggle scene on Blood Mountain was an exact match to the puncture marks found in Cheryl Dunlap's slashed tire.

Faced with overwhelming evidence for kidnapping and the high probability of multiple murder charges across states — potentially involving the death penalty — Hilton's resolve finally broke. His lawyer negotiated a deal: in exchange for leading investigators to Meredith Emerson's body and providing a full confession, the state of Georgia would take the death penalty off the table. Hilton agreed.

Over hours of recorded interviews, Gary Hilton presented a complex and often contradictory self-image in his interviews, revealing a worldview steeped in cynicism, perceived superiority, and detachment from societal norms. He portrayed himself as a philosopher, soldier, scientist, and artist, framing even extreme acts, like pulling out his own teeth, as both practical intimidation and an "artistic-philosophical statement." He viewed ordinary people as shallow, labeling them "posers" or "schmuck townspeople," and believed his intelligence came from reflection rather than formal education. A preoccupation with death, which he traced to age four, underpinned his view that most human neuroses stemmed from existential anxiety.

Hilton expressed profound alienation, identifying as a loner and a sociopath, describing himself as a "round peg in a square hole" unable to find satisfaction in human relationships. His bond with animals, first manifested in the dog he acquired at twenty-one, was far stronger than any with humans, a distinction highlighted in his care for Meredith Emerson's dog Ella even while he abducted and ultimately murdered her. His views on women were harsh and misogynistic; he described them as manipulative, greedy, and heartless, using their sexuality to control men while retaining a nurturing instinct only for children and animals.

Eventually, Gary Michael Hilton laid bare the chilling details of Meredith Emerson's abduction and murder. He described encountering Meredith on the trail, drawn initially by their dogs meeting. He admitted forming the intent to abduct her almost immediately, driven, he claimed, solely by the desire to obtain her ATM card and PIN. He recounted the violent struggle when he confronted her, producing first the knife, then the baton, both of which she bravely fought him for. He admitted to beating her severely to gain control, described securing her first with zip ties, then with a nylon cord leash around her neck, and leading her off the trail. He detailed retrieving her purse from her car, securing her with chains in his van, and his surprising decision to go back for her dog, Ella, because Meredith was voicing concerns.

He described the subsequent days, driving around North Georgia, making repeated, failed attempts to use her ATM cards as Meredith deliberately gave him incorrect PINs — a desperate strategy that likely prolonged her life. He spoke of camping with her in Dawson Forest, bizarrely insisting she was "at ease" and "having a good time," even going hiking with him, despite being his captive. Finally, he recounted the horrifying end. Believing he was about to release her, he led her into a secluded part of the woods, secured her to a tree with a chain, returned to his van for coffee and the iron handle from a car jack, then walked back and brutally bludgeoned her to death. He confessed to decapitating her afterward, claiming it was purely for "forensic" reasons to prevent fiber transfer from her hair, and to pouring bleach over her body to destroy DNA evidence. He admitted he knew from the moment he abducted her that he would have to kill her, and described the act of killing and decapitation as "dreadful," "surrealistic," and like an "out-of-body experience," something so horrific he had to go on "autopilot" to complete it.

Following his confession, Hilton led investigators through the dark woods of Dawson Forest directly to Meredith's mutilated body and, separately, to where he had disposed of her head. On January 31, 2008, less than a month after his arrest, Gary Michael Hilton pleaded guilty to the murder of Meredith Emerson and was sentenced to life in prison without the possibility of parole.

But Hilton's reign of terror extended beyond Meredith and Cheryl. During his interviews, he alluded to his "rampage" starting earlier. A federal investigation soon connected him to the disappearance of John and Irene Bryant, a retired couple from North Carolina who went missing while hiking in Pisgah National Forest in October 2007. Hilton later confessed to these murders as well. He admitted to accosting the couple, demanding their credit cards, beating John with his baton when he refused, and killing Irene on the spot. He then kidnapped John, forced him to withdraw $300 from an ATM (captured on surveillance footage wearing the same yellow jacket), drove him to Nantahala National Forest, and shot him in the head. In 2011, Hilton was indicted in federal court for the Bryant murders, ultimately pleading guilty in 2012 and receiving four additional consecutive life sentences.

He was also considered a suspect in the 2005 disappearance of Rossana Miliani, another hiker who vanished from North Carolina after being seen with an older man matching Hilton's description. However, when detectives interviewed him about her case, Hilton vehemently denied involvement, and a polygraph test indicated no deception, though the reliability of such tests is questionable.

Finally, Hilton faced trial in Florida for the murder of Cheryl Dunlap. Despite his earlier agreement in Georgia, he pleaded not guilty. The prosecution presented the damning evidence: Cheryl's DNA in his van, his DNA on the cigarette butt at the campsite where her likely remains were found, the ATM footage, and the puncture marks on her tire matching his knife. They also played excerpts from his own bizarre home videos, recorded just days after Cheryl vanished, where he seemed to ramble about killing someone. In April 2011, the jury found him guilty of first-degree murder, kidnapping, and grand theft. Gary Michael Hilton, the man who fancied himself a lone wolf philosopher-artist living outside society's rules, was sentenced to death. His "rampage," as he called it, born of a chilling blend of sociopathy, misogyny, and perceived existential insight, left a trail of terror across the national forests of the southeastern United States, a brutal counterpoint to the natural beauty he claimed to cherish.

11

THE VAN IN THE DRIVEWAY

On September 11th, 2021, police officers in Northport, Florida, pulled up to a quiet, suburban home, the residence of the Laundrie family due to an urgent call. They were investigating the disappearance of twenty-two-year-old Gabby Petito, and this house was their only solid lead. They did not have a warrant, but they did not need one to see what was parked in the driveway: a white 2012 Ford Transit van. It was instantly recognizable as the vehicle Gabby had meticulously converted into a DIY camper, the mobile home that was supposed to carry her and her fiancé, Brian Laundrie, on a dream road trip across the country.

When investigators spoke with Brian's parents, Christopher and Roberta Laundrie, the conversation was brief and cold. They insisted they had no idea where their future daughter-in-law was. They did, however, know where their son was: inside the house. The admission was a shock to the officers because the van and Brian were here, but Gabby was not. The simple question hung in the air: Why? When the officers asked to speak with Brian, the Laundries offered no explanations. Instead, they handed over the contact information for their family's lawyer. With no warrant, the police were stonewalled, forced to leave with more questions than they had arrived with. Why did this family already have legal representation? What were they hiding?

The police, however, were not the first to be met with this suspicious, uncooperative silence. The day before, Gabby's mother, Nicole Schmidt, was descending into a state of panic. She had not heard from her daughter in two weeks. She sent a text message to Brian's mother, Roberta, pleading for information: Was Gabby okay? The message was marked as "read," but no reply came. Nicole waited, trying to give Roberta the benefit of the doubt, but when she followed up, the message status turned a stark, definitive green. She had been blocked. Roberta Laundrie had seen the pleas from Gabby's mother and had actively, deliberately, cut off all communication. Gabby's father, Joe Petito, also tried to contact Brian's parents and his sister, Cassie, but was met with the same impenetrable silence. Joe's final, desperate message warned them that if they refused to respond, he would be forced to call the police. The threat was met with nothing.

This behavior was a terrifying betrayal to Gabby's parents, who had, despite their reservations, entrusted their daughter to this family. Gabby had introduced Brian to them in 2019. He seemed quiet, a subdued counterpart to Gabby's vibrant, outgoing personality. When she announced her intention to move in with him and his parents in Northport, they hesitated, gently warning her that the relationship was moving too quickly. But Gabby was determined. In December 2019, she packed up her life in New York and moved over a thousand miles south, taking a leap of faith to begin a new chapter with Brian.

Frustrated and terrified, Nicole Schmidt turned to the only tool she had left: the internet. She created a "Where's Gabby" poster using a joyful, recent picture from the road trip and shared it on Facebook. Gabby had already cultivated a decent following on Instagram by documenting her travels, and the missing person post began to circulate quickly. The next day, September 11th, her parents officially filed a missing person's report in New York. After the Northport police were rebuffed at the Laundrie home, they learned the most critical piece of information: Brian hadn't just returned. He had been back in Florida, with Gabby's van but without Gabby, since September 1st. He had been home for ten days and said nothing, while Gabby's parents were sick with worry. Gabby's parents immediately demanded that the police seize their daughter's van as evidence. This time, the Laundries had no choice but to comply.

On September 12th, the FBI formally opened an investigation, coordinating a wide search in the areas where Gabby was last known to be: Grand Teton National Park and the Bridger-Teton National Forest in Wyoming. The following day, Gabby's parents held a press conference, their faces etched with strain as they revealed the distressing timeline of their last communications. Her father, Joe, confirmed she was in Utah on August 21st. The couple then traveled to Grand Teton, where Gabby FaceTimed her parents on August 25th. That was the last time they ever heard her voice. Her mother, Nicole, received a text from Gabby's phone on August 27th. Then, after three agonizing days of silence, a final, strange text arrived on August 30th. It read, "Can you help Stan? I just keep getting his voicemails and missed calls."

To an outsider, the message may have seemed innocuous, but for Nicole, it was a blaring alarm bell. Stan was Gabby's grandfather, but she had never once in her life referred to him by his first name; he was, and always had been, "Grandpa." Nicole shared her chilling fear with the media, stating plainly, "I don't know if that was her texting me or not."

The press conference ignited a digital wildfire. A new subreddit, "Gabby Petito," was created and quickly had 90,000 members in a single week. This online community became a virtual command center, a massive, crowdsourced detective agency dedicated to compiling information, discussing the case, and inevitably, speculating. The primary focus of that speculation was the absolute, deafening silence from Brian Laundrie and his family. Their refusal to provide any answers soon led to real-world consequences, as protestors gathered outside their Northport home, their voices rising in anger, shouting for Brian to come out and tell them where Gabby was.

Online, users tirelessly debated the family's cold behavior. Some suggested their attorney had simply advised them to invoke their Fifth Amendment right to remain silent. But others countered this argument forcefully, pointing out that while Brian had the right to silence, his complete lack of any apparent desire to help find his missing fiancée was, in itself, a damning admission. He was the only person on Earth who could provide answers, and he was choosing to hide behind his parents and his lawyer.

On September 15th, law enforcement made it official, formally naming Brian Laundrie a person of interest in Gabby's disappearance.

In response, Brian's lawyer, Steven Bertolino, released a statement that only poured gasoline on the fire. He explained that "intimate partners are often the first people law enforcement focuses their attention on" and that "any statement made will be used against you," regardless of his client's involvement. He concluded that on the advice of counsel, Mr. Laundrie would not be speaking. People saw the statement as cold, insensitive, and strategically evasive. It never once flatly denied that his client knew where Gabby was.

With direct communication rendered impossible, Gabby's family took their plea to the national stage. On September 16th, their lawyer stood before a bank of news cameras and read aloud a letter addressed directly to Christopher and Roberta Laundrie. "We believe you know the location where Brian left Gabby," the letter began. "We beg you to tell us. As a parent, how could you let us go through this pain and not help us?" The family's words were heavy with grief, reminding the Laundries that Gabby had lived with them for over a year and was set to become their daughter-in-law. "All we want is Gabby to come home," it concluded. "Please help us make that happen."

That same day, the case grew infinitely more complicated. The Moab City Police Department in Utah released bodycam footage from August 12th, just two weeks before Gabby's last known communication. Officers Danielle Robbins and Eric Pratt had pulled over Gabby's white van after a 911 call reported a domestic dispute — specifically, a man hitting a woman outside a food co-op. The footage was difficult to watch. It showed the officers separating the couple; Brian appeared preternaturally calm, while Gabby was a wreck, visibly shaking, crying, and distraught. She admitted to striking Brian and described being in a state of high stress, referencing her obsessive-compulsive disorder (OCD). Instead of probing deeper or treating the incident as a potential domestic abuse case, the officers ruled it a "mental health crisis." Their solution was to separate the couple for the night, sending Brian to a hotel and leaving a vulnerable, weeping Gabby alone in the van.

The footage went viral, and the officers faced a tidal wave of criticism. Viewers felt that if the police had truly deemed it a mental health crisis, Gabby should have been offered a hospital visit, not abandoned in the van. While some users speculated that Gabby may have been the aggressor, pointing to scratches on Brian's face, most found her behavior inconsistent with that of an abuser. They noted how she immediately took all the blame and belittled herself, while Brian seemed to be putting on a charming, calculated act for the officers. Then, the online sleuths noticed a glaring omission: there were two officers at the stop, but only one officer's footage had been released. They began to demand, loudly, that the Moab Police release Officer Pratt's footage, speculating that it contained something the department was trying to hide.

Just as the public was dissecting this disturbing video, Brian's family dropped their bombshell. On September 17th, they called the police, not with information, but with another disappearance: Brian Laundrie was missing. The news exploded online, with the public immediately voicing suspicion that he had not gone "missing" but had fled. It was then revealed that police had made a critical surveillance error. Investigators had mistakenly believed Brian was still at home because they had seen him drive off in his gray Mustang on September 13th and then saw the same car return on September 15th. They had confidently, and incorrectly, reported to the press that he was accounted for. It turned out the person who drove the car back was not Brian, but his mother, Roberta, her face partially obscured by a baseball cap.

This revelation raised a new, urgent set of questions. If Brian had been missing since the 13th, why did his parents wait until the 17th to report it — two full days after they had retrieved his car and, with it, his only means of transportation home? The Laundries claimed Brian had gone hiking in the nearby Myakkahatchee Creek Environmental Park, which borders the sprawling, 25,000-acre (about 101 square kilometers) Carlton Reserve. They said he often went there for a few days at a time to "unwind," but this time he had not returned. The location itself was forbidding — a wild, swampy, and vast expanse of Florida wilderness, an impenetrable labyrinth of dense brush, water moccasins, and alligators. A local rancher assisting with the search stated bluntly that no one could survive out there for two weeks on foot. This led to widespread speculation that the parents had pointed police to the uninhabitable reserve as a diversion, a way to fake his death and help him escape.

The official timeline was later clarified. The family's attorney, Bertolino, had in fact informed the FBI on the morning of September 14th that Brian had not returned home. It was the FBI, seeing Roberta drive the car back on the 15th, who mistakenly assumed he had returned. The family had reportedly gone to the park on the 14th, found the Mustang, and left it there for Brian. When he still hadn't returned the next day, they found the car ticketed and drove it home to prevent it from being towed.

With both Gabby and Brian now missing, investigators were desperate for leads and pleaded with the public to use the dedicated tip line. The online community mobilized, and the line was flooded with hundreds of tips per day. Amidst a torrent of false sightings and misinformation from people seemingly chasing online clout, a few credible, chilling witness accounts emerged. A woman named Nina Angelo reported seeing a couple she later identified as Gabby and Brian at the Merry Piglets Tex-Mex restaurant in Jackson, Wyoming, on August 27th — the last day Gabby's phone had contact with her mother. She described Gabby as visibly distressed and crying, while her partner was aggressive, pacing in and out of the restaurant and lashing out at the staff.

Another witness, Jessica Schultz, reported seeing the white van multiple times. On August 26th, she was driving behind it on a road in Grand Teton National Park. She saw it again, parked at a trail in Spread Creek, on the evenings of August 27th and 28th, noting it appeared to be empty. She later recognized the van from the Moab bodycam footage because of a distinctive straw hat on the dashboard, and she urged the FBI to search Spread Creek.

Then, a series of sightings placed Brian alone. On August 29th, Miranda Baker and her boyfriend picked up Brian Laundrie near Colter Bay. He told them his fiancée was back at their van working on social media content and offered them $200 for a ride to Jackson. However, when Miranda mentioned their destination was Jackson Hole, Brian "panicked" and insisted they drop him off immediately near Jackson Lake Dam. Shortly after, another driver, Norma Gene Jalivc, picked him up. He again asked for a ride to Jackson but, learning she was going the opposite way, insisted she drop him at the Spread Creek campsite where his fiancée was supposedly waiting. As she approached the entrance to the park, Brian jumped out of the car before it had even fully stopped, seemingly desperate that she not drive all the way in.

These witness accounts were compounded by the release of the original 911 call from Moab, which confirmed the caller's report: "We drove by and the gentleman was slapping the girl." This directly contradicted the narrative the officers had constructed, in which Gabby was the primary aggressor. But the most pivotal clue, the one that would break the case open, came not from a witness but from a camera lens. A traveling couple, Kyle and Jen Bethune, who documented their trips on YouTube, were reviewing their footage from late August. As they scanned their video from the evening of August 27th, they spotted it: Gabby's white Ford Transit van, parked in the Spread Creek dispersed camping area. This footage corroborated Jessica Schultz's sighting and gave investigators a precise, time-stamped location to focus their search.

On the second day of the FBI's intensive search in Spread Creek, they found a body. It was located just off a gravel road, not buried or hidden, but simply left there, abandoned to the elements. It was the moment the entire nation had been dreading. Gabby's stepfather, Jim Schmidt, who had flown to Wyoming to assist in the search, was the first to be contacted. The officers did not need to show him the body; they only had to describe the sweater she was found in. He knew, instantly, that it was her. On September 21st, the FBI made the official, heartbreaking announcement. The Teton County Coroner confirmed the remains belonged to Gabrielle Petito. The initial determination was homicide. The final autopsy would later confirm the cause of death as blunt force injuries to the head and neck, with manual strangulation.

The world's worst fears were confirmed. Gabby had been murdered, and the only person who knew the full story was gone. The following day, a federal arrest warrant was issued for Brian Laundrie. It was not for murder but for the use of unauthorized access devices. He had used Gabby's debit card between August 30th and September 1st, withdrawing about $1,000. As the manhunt for Brian reached a fever pitch, neighbors of the Laundries revealed a shocking detail: after Brian returned home alone, his parents had taken him on a family camping trip to Fort De Soto Park from September 6th to 7th, acting as if nothing was wrong. This discovery led to rampant speculation that the trip was a ruse to destroy evidence, including Gabby's missing cell phone.

On October 1st, the public finally saw why the Moab police had been so reluctant to release the second officer's bodycam footage. The new video showed Officer Pratt asking Gabby if the 911 report of Brian hitting her was true. Through heartbreaking sobs, she replied, "I guess, yeah, but I hit him first." She then added the crucial, whispered detail: "Well, he grabbed my face." The footage also captured the officers laughing about the incident with Brian, commiserating with him, and mocking Gabby's obvious distress. The disparity in treatment was chilling.

Meanwhile, the search for Brian in the Myakkahatchee and Carlton reserves had become a waterlogged, seemingly impossible task. Relentless rainstorms had submerged the entire area under water. Then, on October 20th, the park finally reopened to the public as the floodwaters began to recede. Brian's parents, Chris and Roberta, informed law enforcement they wanted to join the search that day. Shortly after they entered the park, the case came to its grim conclusion. Chris Laundrie ventured off the trail and found a dry bag belonging to his son. At roughly the same time, in a different area, authorities located a second, water-damaged backpack near human skeletal remains. Also at the scene were a rusted revolver, a white metal ring, and a wilted notebook. The remains showed a clear bullet wound to the skull. The following day, dental records confirmed the remains were Brian Laundrie's. His death was officially deemed self-inflicted.

Investigators hoped the notebook, damaged but partially legible, would provide the final answers. Inside, Brian had written his final, self-serving story. He claimed the death was an "unexpected tragedy." He wrote that while rushing to cross Spread Creek, Gabby fell and was gravely injured. He claimed she had a growing bump on her forehead, was freezing cold, and was "begging for an end to her pain." "I ended her life," he wrote. "I thought it was merciful, that it is what she wanted."

This confession, however, was immediately scrutinized and dismantled by the public and investigators, who found it riddled with glaring inconsistencies. The couple was not far from their van, and cell service was available in the area; he could have called 911. Furthermore, the severe injuries he described in the note were not found in Gabby's autopsy report. The timeline also directly contradicted his story. Gabby's last text and laptop activity on the night of August 27th indicated she was alive and well in the van, not dying of injuries in a creek. The very next day, August 28th, Brian was already on the phone with his parents and hiring a lawyer. He was also discovered to have been texting himself between his and Gabby's phones in an attempt to create a false alibi. He sent the deceptive "Stan" text on August 30th and used her card to Zelle himself $700 with the note, "Goodbye, Brian." The evidence was overwhelming: his confession was a lie, crafted to paint a killer as a merciful partner.

While the case was officially closed, several mysteries lingered, fueling continued online debate. Some theories suggested Brian had faked his death, though these were largely disproven by the DNA analysis and the advanced decomposition of the remains, which was consistent with being submerged in a swamp for weeks. A more persistent theory, one publicly shared by Gabby's own mother, was that Brian's parents were somehow involved in his death. Suspicion centered on the fact that his remains were found so quickly on the very day his parents joined the search. This, however, was likely a grim coincidence, as the floodwaters had only just receded that day, finally making the previously inaccessible area searchable.

One discrepancy, however, remains stubbornly unexplained. The autopsy determined the fatal gunshot wound was to Brian's left side. Yet, according to his sister and autopsy confirmations, Brian was right-hand dominant. A retired FBI agent, Jennifer Coffender, commented that this was "bothersome" and statistically inconsistent with a self-inflicted wound. She offered three possibilities: Brian was ambidextrous, he was holding something in his right hand, or the gun was held by someone else.

The suspicion surrounding the Laundries was further cemented by the discovery of an undated letter from Roberta to Brian, found among his belongings from the van. The letter was ominously marked "Burn after reading." In it, she made a dark promise: "If you're in jail, I will bake a cake with a file in it. If you need to dispose of a body, I will show up with a shovel and garbage bags." Roberta insisted the letter was written long before the trip and had no connection to Gabby. While the Petito family lawyer argued the content suggested it was written after the murder, its location in the van's belongings makes it more likely it was written before. Regardless of the timing, the letter demonstrated a chilling, enabling attitude that many felt explained the family's actions.

In the aftermath, the Petito family filed a $3 million wrongful death settlement, which was approved in November 2022. A separate civil suit against the Laundries for emotional distress, claiming they knew Brian had murdered Gabby while they were issuing messages of hope, was settled privately. Every dollar recovered from these lawsuits went directly to the Gabby Petito Foundation.

Gabby Petito's family created a foundation after her death to support searches for missing persons from overlooked communities and assist survivors of domestic violence. Her case's intense media attention had revealed that many other missing persons were previously ignored, highlighting disparities in law enforcement focus. In 2024, the Gabby Petito Act was enacted in Florida, requiring officers to conduct standardized lethality assessments during domestic violence calls — a measure that came too late for Gabby but aims to protect others in her memory.

12

THE WORM THAT TURNED

On the outside, they were the perfect family. Rahan Arshad was a thirty-six-year-old taxi driver, a husband, and a father of three young children who filled their quiet home in Cheadle Hulme, Manchester, with laughter. But behind the closed doors of the house on Turves Road, a different story was unfolding. It was a narrative poisoned by jealousy, paranoia, and a suffocating need for control, one that was about to explode into one of the most shocking family murders in modern British history.

The end began on July 28th, 2006. On that day, Rahan Arshad, consumed by a rage he had been nurturing for years, picked up a rounder's bat. He first went to the bedroom, where he confronted his thirty-two-year-old wife, Uzma Rahan. He bludgeoned her to death, striking her with such ferocity — more than twenty-three times — that investigators would later describe it as one of the most brutal domestic killings they had ever witnessed. His violence, however, was not over. He then went to his children and brought eleven-year-old Adam, eight-year-old Abbas, and six-year-old Henna downstairs to their playroom and, one by one, beat them to death with the same bat.

After slaughtering his entire family, Arshad did not panic. He did not call the police. Instead, he calmly packed his bags, cleaned his car, and drove to London's Heathrow Airport. He had planned his escape with chilling foresight. More than two weeks earlier, he had booked a one-way ticket to Thailand. The day before the murders, he had purchased the rounder's bat. He had even told his family and friends that he was taking Uzma and the children on holiday to Dubai. This lie was his final, cruel masterstroke. On Saturday, July 29th, he boarded his flight and fled the country, leaving the bodies of his wife and three children to decompose inside the sealed family home.

For nearly four weeks, the house on Turves Road stood silent. Neighbors noticed the family was gone but assumed they were on their promised holiday in Dubai. Friends wondered why Uzma, who was normally so communicative, had not called. But as August wore on, a foul stench began to emanate from the property, a smell so overpowering it finally led concerned neighbors to contact the police.

On Sunday, August 20th, 2006, officers arrived and forced their way inside. They were met with a nightmare frozen in time. The bodies of Uzma, Adam, Abbas, and Henna were discovered where they had been slain. They were so badly decomposed after weeks in the summer heat that police would need to use dental records just to formally confirm their identities. The devastating murders of a mother and her three children shocked the entire community.

An immediate manhunt was launched for Rahan Arshad, who was now the sole suspect. Police discovered his BMW 320 car abandoned at Heathrow Airport, confirming he had fled the country. Detectives from Greater Manchester Police, working with Interpol, quickly traced his flight to Bangkok, Thailand. They issued an international appeal, and Arshad's own brother, Razan, made a public plea for him to surrender.

The search intensified, with authorities in Thailand on high alert. The breakthrough came on August 30th, 2006, just over a month after the murders. Rahan Arshad was questioned by Thai authorities at the Thai-Malaysian border as he was attempting to re-enter Thailand. He agreed to return to the United Kingdom voluntarily and was flown from Bangkok to Heathrow, where he was met by detectives as he stepped off the plane. He was immediately arrested on suspicion of four counts of murder and transported to Manchester for questioning.

Upon his arrest, Arshad displayed no hint of remorse. His confession to the officers was calm and detached, leaving no doubt about his guilt. He admitted to the murders in chillingly vulgar terms, expressing brief sorrow only for his children before reverting to cold indifference. Detectives later noted that this fleeting moment was the only sign of emotion he ever showed. Afterward, he refused to answer any further questions.

His trial at Manchester Crown Court began in early 2007. Despite his initial confession, Arshad pleaded not guilty to all four counts of murder. He presented the jury with a desperate, fabricated story: he claimed he had returned home to find that his wife, Uzma, had bludgeoned their three children to death, and that he, in a fit of rage, had then killed her.

The prosecution systematically dismantled his defense, painting a portrait not of a grieving father, but of a cold and calculating killer. The jury heard how Arshad had been consumed by jealousy. During his own testimony, Arshad claimed he was "the worm that turned," attempting to portray himself as a long-suffering victim. He described his wife as a "bad-tempered, materialistic spendaholic" who constantly put him down and thought herself superior. He said he struggled to keep her in the lifestyle she demanded, working long hours as a private hire driver. He told the jury he "adored her," but his words were laced with resentment and a deep-seated need for control.

He grew increasingly angry over her new preference for Western-style clothing, often criticizing her for wearing tight jeans and tops, which he claimed were inappropriate for a Pakistani mother. Their marriage — an arranged union between first cousins who had never met before — had long been troubled. His paranoia focused on the belief that Uzma was being unfaithful. He said his suspicions began when she received phone calls during shopping trips and told the caller she couldn't talk because she was with her husband. Uzma, who worked part-time as a beautician, maintained that these were simply work-related calls. Arshad later claimed to have seen text messages that confirmed his fears, though she continued to deny any affair.

The court learned that his paranoia was, in fact, based in reality. Uzma had indeed begun an affair with a neighbor's husband, a man named

Nikki. But the affair was a symptom of a marriage that was already broken, largely by Arshad's own actions. In February 2004, while Uzma was in Pakistan grieving the death of her father, Arshad decided to "teach her a lesson." He sold their family home, flew to Lahore, dumped their three children with her, and then filed fake divorce papers before going traveling. He even allegedly married another woman, a claim he denied in court. He would later admit this was a big, massive mistake.

After his travels, Arshad claimed he wanted a reconciliation. Uzma's brother, Rahhat Ali, acted as a mediator, and Arshad agreed to buy a new house on Turves Road, putting the property in both their names. But the reconciliation was a sham, a final, desperate act of control. He embarked on a lavish spending spree to win her back, but his gestures were empty and laced with deceit. He bought a £30,000 (about $35,000) BMW 320, telling Uzma it was an early birthday present. In reality, he had bought it on hire-purchase, paid only one installment, and insured it solely in his own name. He bought a new computer for the children, gold jewelry for his wife, and redecorated the house with new wardrobes and carpets.

The sudden burst of generosity did nothing to ease Uzma's fears. She wasn't confused — she was frightened. To those closest to her, she revealed her growing dread, her words carrying an eerie sense of inevitability. She told friends that her husband had either truly changed or was on the verge of killing her. To one, she said grimly, "Count the days until he kills me."

The prosecution presented the jury with the evidence of his cold premeditation: the rounder's bat purchased the day before the killings, and the plane ticket to Thailand booked two weeks in advance. The jury did not believe his story for a second. On March 13th, 2007, Rahan Arshad was found guilty on all four counts of murder.

When the verdicts were announced, the courtroom was heavy with emotion. In the public gallery, Uzma's mother and two brothers sat together, their grief and anger barely contained. Her brother, Rahhat Ali, cried out as the guilty verdict was delivered, his voice breaking the tense silence. Judge David Clark addressed Arshad directly, calling the evidence against him "overwhelming." He condemned Arshad's actions as acts of "great brutality," describing how he had beaten his wife to death in their bedroom before coldly leading his sleepy children downstairs to kill them as well. The judge noted there was no indication of mental illness, declaring that life imprisonment would truly mean life. Rahan Arshad was sentenced to spend the rest of his days behind bars, with no possibility of release.

After the hearing, Detective Superintendent Martin Bottomley, who led the investigation, called the case one of the most brutal and devastating murders he had ever encountered. He then read a statement from Uzma's grieving family, their words capturing the depth of their loss. They spoke of Uzma as a best friend, a beloved sister, and a devoted daughter whose absence had left a void no one could fill. Her mother, they said, could not comprehend how Arshad could destroy the very family he was meant to protect. The statement ended with a final, resolute sentiment — relief that justice had ensured he would never walk free again.

The murders sent shockwaves through the community, leaving friends and neighbors struggling to comprehend the horror that had unfolded behind closed doors. To those who knew the family, Arshad had always appeared to be a devoted husband and a doting father who adored his children. His closest friend told reporters he could not believe Arshad was capable of violence, insisting there was "no way he would ever hurt those kids." At the school where Uzma worked as a dinner lady and where the children were pupils, the grief was equally profound. Staff and parents remembered the children as kind and well-mannered, and Uzma as a respected, gentle woman who brightened the lives of those around her.

Behind the facade of a happy, ordinary household lay a man consumed by jealousy, paranoia, and a desire for absolute control — an obsession that culminated in one of the most horrific family murders in modern British history. The brutality of his actions, the calculated planning, and the cold detachment he displayed left a community reeling and a family irreparably shattered. For Uzma, Adam, Abbas, and Henna, there was no escape from the violence within their own home. For Arshad, justice was swift and unyielding, ensuring he would never have the opportunity to harm again. The case would leave an enduring mark, not only on the city of Manchester but on all who struggle to understand how a man so seemingly ordinary could commit such an unspeakable atrocity.

13

THE YERBA BUENA CULT

Yerba Buena, a communal farming settlement at the edge of the Sierra Madre in the early 1960s, was small enough that a newcomer's footsteps carried. Fewer than a hundred people lived there, arranged in a handful of families who had been sent to establish cropland for the state of Guanajuato. The village had no police post, no school, no phones, no electricity, and no formal government presence. People were skilled at agriculture and short on money, literacy, and outside contact. In 1962, brothers Santos and Cayetano Hernández arrived as strangers and immediately became the center of attention because strangers were rare. They had spent years roaming Mexico with petty frauds and amateur magic, and they had decided they wanted something larger and more lucrative. In Yerba Buena, they saw isolation and vulnerability and moved to occupy the space.

The brothers announced that they were prophets of ancient gods and that the community had been chosen. If everyone obeyed, the gods would reveal treasure hidden in the nearby mountains; if anyone refused, the gods would punish heresy. The promise made use of a popular regional myth about gold in the hills. To dress the claim, the brothers performed simple stagecraft, the same sleights of hand they had used to sell smaller cons elsewhere. The villagers, who already believed in the possibility of treasure, turned over their savings and personal valuables and installed the men in the best hut, at the mouth of a cave that would become the center of ritual life. In short order, the brothers were being fed and waited upon. Money was thin in Yerba Buena, and the initial take disappointed them. They pivoted to sex and control.

Santos and Cayetano began selecting girls — typically fourteen to sixteen — and told parents that the gods had commanded sexual initiation as part of divine instruction. The girls were abused and then sold into brothels in nearby towns, generating cash. The brothers also forced adult women and some men to serve as sex slaves. With their authority fixed in daily life, they moved the community's focus into the cave and built a pattern of ceremonies: incense and chants, peyote tea passed from hand to hand, marijuana smoke, the slaughter of a goat by throat-cutting, and then an orgy conducted on the cave floor. The setting was damp and dark, and the logic was simple — ritual obedience would bring treasure.

As weeks passed without the promised reward, villagers began to talk. Doubt spread quietly, and word reached the brothers. They needed to pull the village back under tight control. They left for Monterrey to see an associate from their trafficking business, a local pimp named Eleazar Solís. The idea was to return to Yerba Buena with a woman who could appear as an incarnate goddess, a living sign that the prophets had, in fact, been in contact with the supernatural. Eleazar said he had someone perfect for the role: his eighteen-year-old sister, Magdalena Solís. There is very little about her early life beyond the fact that she had been forced into sex work at twelve and that she sometimes worked as a fortune-teller and medium, selling contact with the dead. The brothers explained the scheme, and Eleazar and Magdalena agreed. A role offering constant deference and a change of circumstances was attractive.

They chose an Aztec figure this time — a correction from the brothers' earlier confusion between Andean and Mesoamerican pantheons — and prepared Magdalena to appear as Coatlicue. They dressed her with a headdress and bones, built the scene, and included Eleazar as "high priest." The brothers, still planning to be ultimate decision-makers, would continue as prophets. On the appointed night the villagers filed into the cave. The familiar sequence began: chanting, incense, peyote. Then a third man announced himself as a high priest of the ancient goddess. Flash powder ignited, smoke filled the cave and when it cleared, Magdalena stood where no one had been a moment before. The villagers fell to their knees, convinced the gods had, at last, responded.

For a short while, the structure remained the same. Magdalena presided over ceremonies that looked like the old ones: drugs, sacrifice, and sex. But the social dynamic changed quickly. Worship and deference concentrated on her. The villagers brought her needs and waited for her in the hut. She took sex slaves for herself. In a matter of days the attention hardened into conviction; she began to believe the role and the chain of command inverted. Instead of advising and directing the pageant from behind the scenes, Santos and Cayetano found themselves on the outside of the true authority. Even Eleazar's claims as brother and handler fell away. Magdalena had the village, and with it the capacity to command.

With that shift came new practices. She replaced peyote tea with blood mixed into a ceremonial cup. At first she cut herself to provide it, blending her blood with the hallucinogen and passing the vessel around. Then the rites changed tone. During ceremonies, she forced participants into acts designed to obliterate taboo: incest, bestiality, sexual assaults on children. The point was not only gratification but proof of control. If she could order what people had never imagined doing and watch them do it, she knew there was nothing beyond her reach. But soon the objections started to come when two villagers questioned the direction of the cult. Not having any of this, Magdalena had them lynched. Their deaths, carried out by their neighbors, reset the terms of disagreement inside a tiny community where every family was tied to every other.

From that moment human sacrifice replaced animal sacrifice. The records are unclear about the numbers, and mostly, identify at least six victims later found dismembered in the caves, with possibilities as high as fifteen or sixteen. Selection was described in two ways by sources: sometimes random, sometimes aimed at those who thought to harbor doubts or plans to leave. However chosen, victims were cut apart, blood was drained, mixed with chicken blood and peyote, and passed to the congregation. Orgies followed. Hearts were torn from chests; in some cases, the victims were still alive when the chest was opened. The cadence of ceremonies settled: assemble, ingest, kill, drink, dismember, copulate, disperse. This phase lasted roughly six weeks.

On the night of May 31, 1963, a fourteen-year-old boy named Sebastián Guerrero was moving through the area around Yerba Buena. He had no connection to the village and knew nothing about the cult. He saw lights flickering in a cave and went to see what was there. As he approached, he heard sounds he later described as part human, part wild animal. Inside, he hid behind a rock and watched a woman at an altar holding what looked like a human heart. People on the floor were engaged in sexual acts. A chalice passed from hand to hand. On the altar lay a dismembered body. When Sebastián understood what he was seeing, he ran, fifteen miles (about twenty-five kilometers) to the nearest police station in Vallegrande and told officers what he had witnessed.

At first the officers doubted the story because it sounded impossible. Sebastián insisted. An officer named Luis Martínez volunteered to check. He and the boy drove toward Yerba Buena and did not return. After a day without contact, colleagues reported Martínez missing and asked the state to open an investigation. Officers canvassed the region's fringe settlements and heard consistent rumors about ancient ceremonies and devil worship in the caves near the village. The pattern in the reports matched Sebastián's account. Police requested military support. A joint force moved on Yerba Buena.

They went straight to the farmhouse where Magdalena and Eleazar were living. Inside, they were found both in bed and heavily intoxicated. Santos ran from the house and a pursuit began. During the exchange of gunfire, police shot and killed him. Searches of the house and grounds found the bodies of Sebastián Guerrero and Officer Luis Martínez. Martínez's chest had been opened and his heart removed. His brother, Cayetano, was already dead, killed by cult member Jesús Rubio, who later said he wanted a piece of the high priest's body as protection. Several cultists who had barricaded themselves inside a cave died in ensuing shootouts.

With the principal figures accounted for, police and soldiers searched the cave complex. They recovered the physical evidence that matched Sebastián's description: ritual arrangements, blood traces, and bodies. Six dismembered victims were found there. The arrests included Magdalena and Eleazar and a number of villagers. Prosecutors sought testimony from members of the cult to build a broad case against the leadership for multiple murders. No one agreed to testify. Whether out of loyalty, fear, or both, the villagers stayed silent. The absence of insider witnesses shaped the charges. Magdalena and Eleazar were tried for the murders of Sebastián Guerrero and Officer Luis Martínez. They were convicted and sentenced to fifty years in prison. Several villagers were convicted of gang murder and lynching and received thirty-year sentences. By the calendar, Magdalena's term would have ended in 2013 but no reliable public update exists on her status; it has been speculated that she died in prison.

What happened in Yerba Buena did not depend on elaborate theology, only on the conviction that an authority stood above question and could be enforced in a dark place at a distance from ordinary scrutiny. The cave was close to the village in miles and far from it in every other way. When soldiers and police walked its floor after the raid and counted bodies, the distance collapsed. Everything that had been done in secrecy was measured. The rest was the work of courts and calendars. The village returned to itself with the knowledge of what had happened inside it. The record that remains is spare: names, places, sequences, sentences — but it is enough.

14

THE MONSTER WITH 21 FACES

The evening of March 18, 1984, began like any other for Katsuhisa Ezaki. As the president of Ezaki Glico, one of Japan's largest and most beloved candy manufacturers, his life was one of success and routine. He was in his home in Osaka, enjoying a quiet evening bath, when that routine was violently interrupted. Two hooded, armed assailants suddenly burst into his home, stormed the bathroom, and kidnapped the naked executive. The audacious crime marked the beginning of a bizarre and theatrical extortion campaign that would baffle Japanese authorities and hold the entire nation in a state of anxious fascination for seventeen months.

The day after the abduction, a ransom note arrived. The demand was staggering: 1 billion yen (about $6.5 million) and 100 kilograms of gold worth about $10 million. The kidnappers specified a drop-off at a particular phone booth, but the elaborate plan collapsed almost immediately. Just two days after his capture, before any money could be paid, Ezaki escaped. In a dramatic account of his break for freedom, he described how he managed to loosen his bindings, break down a door of the isolated warehouse where he was being held, and find two railroad employees who helped him contact the police. He was still wearing the clothes his assailants had given him. While Ezaki was safe, the ordeal was far from over. He had no idea who his captors were, and they, it turned out, were just getting started.

Though their initial kidnapping plot had failed, the perpetrators simply shifted their tactics. They issued a new demand for $480,000, but this time, the threat was aimed not just at the company's president, but at the public itself. If the money was not paid, they would begin poisoning Glico candies with potassium cyanide. To prove their seriousness, the group reportedly snuck into Glico headquarters and set some of the property on fire. The escalation from a targeted kidnapping to a threat of mass public poisoning was a shocking development, one that left authorities scrambling.

Despite the growing list of crimes, authorities were at a loss. In the Japan of the 1980s, an unsolved case of this magnitude was a rarity and a professional embarrassment. The Japanese police force was famously effective; in 1983, they had solved 97.1% of all murder cases and 55.3% of thefts, statistics that dwarfed the clearance rates in the United States. Failing to get to the bottom of the Glico case was seen as a public failure, a "black eye" on the police's stellar reputation. The *Yomiuri* newspaper ran an editorial that captured the growing public sentiment, stating, "We do not recall a case in which criminals have made such fools of the police."

Perhaps no one was more frustrated by the police's incompetence than the criminals themselves. On April 8, 1984, the press received the first of what would become over 100 letters sent over the next year and a half. The letter was a masterpiece of public taunting, addressed "To the stupid police." It openly mocked their efforts, asking if they were idiots and stating that if they were professionals, the case would already be solved. Because the police had such a high handicap, the letter offered to provide some hints. The writers proceeded to debunk the prevailing theories, clarifying that the kidnapping was not an inside job and that the owners of the warehouse Ezaki escaped from were not involved. They even offered new clues, stating that the car they used was gray and naming the grocery store where they bought their food. The letter ended with a final barb, suggesting that if the police could not catch them with this much information, they were just thieves of taxpayer money, and perhaps the criminals should kidnap the head of the prefectural police instead.

The letters continued to pour in, each one a public performance. Critics at the time categorized the group's actions as *gekijo hanzai*, or "crime as theater." The group had a brilliant knack for capturing public attention and leveraged the media to ensure their threats and taunts were widely reported. The letters often provided seemingly specific but ultimately useless details, such as the exact gate they used to enter a factory or the model of typewriter they were using. None of the clues ever led to a breakthrough, and all the physical evidence left at the crime scenes was either stolen or mass-produced, rendering it untraceable. The police looked more and more incompetent. The only clue that seemed to hold any weight was linguistic; the dialect used in the letters pointed to someone from the Osaka region. But this theory, while interesting, did not bring authorities any closer to an arrest.

By June of 1984, the criminals had given themselves a name, one drawn directly from Japanese popular fiction. In their letters, they began referring to themselves as *Kainin Nijūichi Mensō* — The Monster with 21 Faces. It was a direct reference to a 1936 children's story by the famed mystery writer Edogawa Rampo, titled "The Mystery Man with the 21 Faces." The name was fitting. Rampo's story featured a master thief who stirred up the newspapers daily and was so adept at disguise that he could be anyone. One excerpt from the story seemed to describe the group's philosophy perfectly. It told of a gang that, without fail, would send a letter of warning announcing the date, place, and object of their planned crime. They did this, the story suggested, either because they did not want an unfair battle or simply to show that no matter how many precautions are taken, they can still commit the crime with their great skill. The fictional thief had become a real-world boogeyman.

After months of tormenting Glico, the Monster with 21 Faces expanded its operations. In September 1984, another major Japanese confectioner, Morinaga & Company, began receiving extortion letters. The group threatened unspecified action if they did not receive $410,000. According to police, Morinaga refused to pay. The Monster's response would be their most terrifying act yet.

On October 8, Japanese newspapers received a chilling new letter, this one addressed "To moms throughout Japan." It began with a mocking tone, noting that in autumn, when appetites are strong, sweets are delicious. It then declared that when thinking of sweets, one thinks of Morinaga. "We've added some special flavor," the letter continued, "The flavor of potassium cyanide is a little bitter." The Monster announced they had placed twenty boxes of these "bitter sweets" in stores from Hakata to Tokyo, and that they had attached a notice on them that they contained poison.

That same day, a frantic search began. Sure enough, packages of Morinaga cookies and candy were discovered in grocery stores across Japan. Attached to them were typewritten labels that read, "Danger. Cyanide!" In total, eighteen packages were found, one in a supermarket just thirty-five yards (about thirty-two meters) from Katsuhisa Ezaki's home. When tested, not all contained cyanide, but at least one was found to contain a lethal dose. Thanks to the warning labels, no one was harmed. But the letter that warned of the tainted sweets also contained a far more sinister threat: the next time, there would be thirty boxes, and they would not be labeled.

The threat of unlabeled, poisoned candy sent a wave of panic across the country. For the next two weekends, a reported 40,000 police officers staked out grocery stores, a massive and desperate mobilization. The stakeouts yielded nothing. Thankfully, it did not appear the group ever went through with their threat of unlabeled poison.

Investigators did, however, find two new potential clues. The first was surveillance video from October 7, the day before the poison letter arrived. It showed a suspect with permed hair, glasses, and a baseball hat placing something on a shelf where poisoned candy was later found. But this promising lead quickly dissolved. The camera was bad, the lighting was poor, and the security tape had not been changed in over a year, resulting in a grainy, useless image. Photos of this "Video Man," as he came to be known, were released to the public, but he was never identified.

The second clue was a set of audio recordings from phone calls attempting to extort money. When released, the public was disturbed to hear that the voices on the tapes were not those of hardened gangsters but of a woman and a child. At one point, the child's voice could be heard giving clear instructions for a money drop, telling the company representative to leave the money "behind the seat of the bus stop bench." The involvement of a woman and child forced everyone to reconsider just who, or what, the Monster with 21 Faces truly was.

By March 1985, a full year after the kidnapping of Ezaki, the list of harassed companies had grown to thirty-one. Japan's finest detectives were still completely baffled. On several occasions, a company would actually pull together the demanded ransom, but the Monster with 21 Faces never picked it up. They seemed to have an uncanny ability to spot a trap. In one instance, the group instructed Glico representatives to wait for a phone call at a specific truck stop. Plainclothes policemen went in their place, but the call never came. The follow-up letter from the Monster was particularly humiliating. They mocked the police for thinking they could be fooled, dressed up in their "nice businessmen's blue suits." The group wrote that they could tell immediately they were cops, that "those shifty eyes gave you away." At every turn, the Monster was one step ahead.

Then, as abruptly as it began, it was over. On August 12, 1985, a year and a half after they first kidnapped a candy man from his bathtub, the Monster with 21 Faces sent their final letter. They announced they were stopping. The case had become one of the largest and most expensive in Japanese history. According to Japan's National Police Agency, authorities had received over 28,000 tips and had utilized over 130,000 police officers in the investigation. And they had nothing.

The economic damage was immense. A year after the kidnapping, the Japanese Ministry of Agriculture claimed sweets consumption across the country was down 10%. Both Ezaki Glico and Morinaga suffered massive losses. After the public poisoning threat, all Glico products were pulled from the shelves, forcing the company to temporarily shut down production and lay off two-thirds of its part-time employees. Morinaga's sales were estimated to have plummeted by as much as 60%. The Monster had failed to collect a single yen in ransom, but they had cost the corporations millions and terrorized the public.

In the aftermath, with a stack of taunting letters and a humiliated police force, theories about the Monster's identity flourished. The first, and one of the most popular at the beginning of the crime wave, was that the entire affair was an inside job, and that Katsuhisa Ezaki himself was in on the plot. This theory was based almost entirely on public disbelief that Ezaki had been able to escape his kidnappers so easily. However, no actual evidence ever surfaced to support this. Furthermore, the theory buckled under logical scrutiny. Glico's business was devastated by the ordeal. It made little sense for Ezaki to orchestrate a scheme that involved setting his own property on fire, pulling all of his products from the shelves, and laying off a huge portion of his workforce.

A second, more compelling theory pointed to an act of long-simmering revenge. Nearly thirty years earlier, in 1955, the Morinaga company had been at the center of a horrific tragedy. A stabilizing agent used in their dry milk product was accidentally contaminated with arsenic. By 1956, over 12,000 infants had been injured and 138 had died from the poisoning. A 1969 report showed that survivors continued to suffer related ailments. By the time the Monster began its campaign in 1984, the survivors of the dry milk incident would have been in their late twenties or early thirties, perhaps, this theory suggested, ready to seek revenge on the company that had poisoned them. This, however, failed to explain the full scope of the crimes. Why would a group seeking revenge on Morinaga target Ezaki Glico first and most aggressively, and why would they go on to harass dozens of other unrelated food companies?

The final and most tantalizing theory centers on a single man: Manabu Miyazaki. In November 1984, a drop of 100 million yen (about $650 million) was arranged in Kyoto. Police surveilling the drop-off spotted a suspicious man, later described as the "fox-eyed man," and gave chase. In what had become a predictable pattern, the suspect eluded capture. The police did, however, find the stolen car he had been driving, and inside was a police scanner, explaining how the group had stayed one step ahead. In January, authorities released a police sketch of the "fox-eyed man." The likeness was reportedly so strong that it led to his identification as Manabu Miyazaki. Even Miyazaki's own mother, who happened to be from Osaka, allegedly believed the sketch was of her son.

Miyazaki fit the profile. He was the son of a yakuza boss, a known criminal who had organized anti-police actions in college and had already been arrested several times. It seemed the police had finally made a face-saving break in the case, but charges were never brought against him. Miyazaki apparently produced a rock-solid alibi, and no hard evidence ever tied him to the case.

Miyazaki would later write a memoir detailing his life of crime. The book was released, perhaps tellingly, shortly after the statute of limitations for the Monster with 21 Faces case had expired. The cover of the book was the very police sketch that had made him famous. Though he confessed to other crimes, Miyazaki never mentioned any involvement in the 21 Faces spree. But in a final, ironic twist, the book went on to earn the known criminal over 100 million yen (about $650 million) — a sum comparable to the ransoms he was suspected of trying to collect.

In the end, the Monster with 21 Faces got away with it. Even with the statute of limitations long expired, no one has ever come forward to claim responsibility. The identities of the group members, their true motives, and the face of the man in the surveillance video all remain a mystery. Unless the real faces behind the crime someday decide to reveal themselves, the case of the Monster with 21 Faces remains one of Japan's most fascinating and audacious unsolved crimes.

15

THE GIRL WHO CARRIED A SKULL

On the crisp, cold morning of January 13, 1995, a husband and wife were out for their routine jog along the wooded trails near the University of Tennessee's agricultural campus in Knoxville. As they moved through the quiet landscape, their conversation was cut short by a jarring sight. Splattered across the path, stark against the dead winter leaves, was something unmistakably red. It was blood. In a more secluded, wooded section of the trail, they saw that the splatters formed a grim path leading away from the trail and into the gray, thickening trees of the park. They called over a nearby groundskeeper, and together, the three of them followed the trail of blood deeper into the woods. It led them to a scene of unimaginable horror. Lying in a muddy clearing was the battered and bloody corpse of a young woman.

The police were called, and the area was quickly cordoned off. The crime scene was extensive, a chaotic tableau of violence. There were signs of a desperate struggle: broken foliage, multiple footprints churned into the mud, and discarded articles of clothing strewn about. A large pool of blood was found about thirty feet (ten meters) from where the body lay, suggesting the victim had been attacked, had managed to fight off her assailants and run, only to be overcome and dragged back to her final resting place. The woman, nude from the waist up, had been subjected to a brutal and prolonged assault. Her head had been bludgeoned, her face and body were covered in cuts, and her throat had been slashed. But it was the final, deliberate mutilation that spoke to a motive beyond simple violence. Carved deep into the victim's chest was a pentagram. This was not just a murder; it was a ritual.

The epicenter of this dark story was the Knoxville Job Corps, a federally funded educational program located just off Dale Avenue. In the mid-1990s, Job Corps centers across the country served as a last chance for young people, typically from low-income or troubled backgrounds, who had dropped out of high school and were seeking a way to get their lives back on track. The Knoxville center, however, had developed a notorious reputation for crime, drugs, and mismanagement. In fact, the murder that January morning would be the final straw, the horrific event that would lead to the center's permanent closure just a few months later. It was this troubled institution that brought together the three central figures of the crime: a victim looking for a future, and two killers bound by a shared obsession with the occult.

Christa Pike was born in West Virginia in March 1976, into a world that offered her little in the way of stability. Her mother was an alcoholic, and her father was largely absent, leaving Christa to be raised by her grandmother. For a time, under her grandmother's care, she was a bright and promising young girl. But when she was twelve, her grandmother passed away, and Christa was forced to return to her mother's chaotic and destructive orbit. Her life quickly spiraled downward. Her mother introduced her to drugs at a young age, she dropped out of school, and she was arrested numerous times for stealing, eventually landing in juvenile detention. But by the time she was seventeen, she claimed she wanted to change her ways. The Job Corps was going to be her path to a different life. She moved to the dorms in Knoxville with the stated goal of studying to become a nurse. In reality, she had little interest in hitting the books. She was far more interested in the social scene, and in one young man in particular.

At the Job Corps center, Christa met and fell deeply in love with Tadaryl Shipp. Like Christa, Tadaryl had a rough upbringing. He had grown up in Memphis, dropped out of school at a young age, and had been involved with gangs. He, too, had come to Job Corps in an effort to turn his life around, enrolling in the culinary arts program with the dream of becoming a chef. But Tadaryl had a dark side, an intense fascination with Satanism, the occult, and all things demonic. He kept a small shrine to Satan in his dorm room, and it was over this shared interest that he and Christa bonded. They became inseparable, attached at the hip, spending their time performing seances, chanting, and poring over occult texts. She became, in her own words, his "little devil." Their twisted romance was the crucible in which the murder would be forged.

Into this volatile mix walked Colleen Slemmer. Originally from Jacksonville, Florida, Colleen did not have the same troubled background as Christa and Tadaryl. She was at Job Corps to study computer technology, a quiet and unassuming nineteen-year-old focused on building a future for herself. But from the moment Colleen arrived, Christa saw her not as a fellow student but as a rival. She became convinced, with a jealousy that quickly festered into paranoid obsession, that Colleen was trying to steal Tadaryl away from her. Colleen and her friends vehemently denied this, but Christa's perception was her reality, and that reality was becoming increasingly violent.

After the students returned from the Christmas break in early 1995, Christa's rage toward Colleen reached a boiling point. On January 11th, she confided in a friend named Kim, telling her that she was going to kill Colleen because, as she put it, "she just felt mean that day." The next day, January 12th, Christa put her plan into motion. She enlisted Tadaryl and another friend, Shidola Peterson — who was also interested in Satanism — to help her. That evening, around 8:00 p.m., the trio lured Colleen away from the dorms with a promise of smoking marijuana together. They walked for about twenty minutes, making their way to the secluded, wooded trails of the nearby university agricultural campus.

Christa would later claim that she had only planned on fighting Colleen, roughing her up a bit to warn her away from Tadaryl. But she admitted to bringing a box cutter with her. Shidola Peterson was posted as a lookout, and in the dark woods, the attack began. It was not a fight; it was a methodical and sadistic torture session that lasted for nearly an hour. Christa and Tadaryl unleashed a torrent of violence on the terrified young woman. As Colleen pleaded for her life, Christa slashed at her with the box cutter and beat her relentlessly. Each time Colleen managed to break free and run, Tadaryl would chase her down and drag her back. At one point, they grabbed a large, heavy chunk of asphalt and slammed it into her head multiple times, fracturing her skull.

According to Shidola, who would later turn state's witness, the attack was not just a spontaneous burst of jealous rage. She testified that days earlier, she had overheard Christa and Tadaryl talking about wanting to perform a human sacrifice for the devil, and Colleen's name had come up. In the woods that night, Christa seemed to be channeling something dark and otherworldly, later claiming that she had heard voices telling her what to do. As Colleen lay dying, Christa and Tadaryl carved the pentagram into her chest. It took a long time for Colleen to die. When it was finally over, Christa took a final, gruesome souvenir: she used a piece of the asphalt to break off a small piece of Colleen's shattered skull, which she wrapped up and put in her pocket.

Around 10:00 p.m., two hours after they had left the dorms, Christa, Tadaryl, and Shidola returned. Colleen was not with them. Later that night, Christa went to her friend Kim's room. In a state of manic excitement, she confessed to the murder, laughing, singing, and dancing as she recounted the horrific details. To prove her story, she proudly showed Kim the piece of Colleen's skull she had taken. Her lack of remorse was absolute and chilling. The very next morning, around the same time that the joggers were discovering Colleen's body, Christa was in the Job Corps cafeteria, brazenly showing off her grisly souvenir to other students while she ate breakfast. She was overheard telling another student, in reference to her shoes, "That's not mud, that's blood." Her complete inability to conceal her crime, or perhaps her overwhelming need to brag about it, would lead to her swift capture. One of the students she had boasted to called their mother, who immediately called the police.

The investigation, which had barely begun at the crime scene, now had a clear direction. Detectives arrived at the Job Corps center and, after confirming that Colleen Slemmer was missing, they consulted the dormitory's sign-out logs. The records showed that Christa, Tadaryl, and Shidola had all checked out and back in at the exact same time on the night of the murder. Colleen had only checked out. On January 15th, the police brought them in for questioning. During a search of their rooms, they found Tadaryl's satanic shrine. Faced with the evidence and the testimony of the students Christa had confessed to, all of them were arrested and charged with first-degree murder. They did not deny their involvement. Christa, in particular, seemed almost proud of what she had done, even walking investigators through the entire event, calmly pointing out where they had dumped Colleen's clothing and identification.

Christa Pike's trial began in March 1996. The prosecution had a mountain of evidence against her, including her own confession and the damning testimony of Shidola Peterson, who had agreed to testify in exchange for a lighter sentence. The defense team tried to argue that Christa was a product of a broken home, a deeply troubled young woman suffering from a host of mental illnesses, including bipolar disorder and post-traumatic stress disorder but any sympathy the jury might have had was erased by the sheer barbarity of the crime and Christa's chilling lack of remorse. On March 22, 1996, after only a few hours of deliberation, the jury found her guilty of both first-degree murder and conspiracy to commit murder. She was sentenced to death by electrocution, becoming the youngest woman in the United States to be sentenced to death at the time.

Days after receiving her death sentence, she sent a letter to Tadaryl, which was intercepted by prison authorities. The letter was a shocking testament to her unrepentant and sociopathic nature. "Hey love," she wrote, "I just want you to know how much I love you... you see what I get for trying to be nice to a hoe? I went ahead and bashed her brains out so she'd die quickly, instead of letting her bleed to death and suffer more... and they fry me. Ain't that stupid?"

Because he was seventeen at the time of the murder, Tadaryl Shipp escaped the death penalty and was sentenced to life in prison with the possibility of parole after twenty-five years. Shidola Peterson, for her cooperation, received six years of probation. Christa Pike was sent to death row, where she has remained for the past quarter of a century, a source of constant trouble and bizarre legal maneuvering. She has filed and withdrawn numerous appeals, at one point even requesting to have her execution date sped up, only to have her attorneys immediately file arguments against it. Her capacity for violence did not end with her incarceration. In August 2001, she attempted to murder a fellow inmate, strangling her with a shoelace, an act for which she received an additional twenty-five-year sentence. In 2012, she was at the center of a foiled escape plot, which involved a former prison guard and another man she had been corresponding with.

Today, Christa Pike remains the only woman on death row in the state of Tennessee. Now in her late forties, she has spent more of her life behind bars than not. In recent interviews, she has expressed a kind of muted regret, stating that she knows she did something horrible and deserves to be in prison for the rest of her life, but that she does not deserve to die. But for the family of Colleen Slemmer, and for a justice system confronted with the sheer, remorseless evil of her crime, any punishment short of the one she was given seems inadequate. The story of Christa Pike is a chilling saga of jealousy, obsession, and a teenage romance that devolved into a ritual of torture and human sacrifice, a crime so brutal that it not only ended a young woman's life but also shuttered an institution and left an indelible stain on the community of Knoxville.

16

HITLER DIARIES

In 1983, one of the most significant and explosive historical discoveries of the twentieth century was presented to the editors of *Stern*, an internationally respected German news magazine. A trusted, longtime journalist on their staff, Gerd Heidemann, brought them two black leather-bound volumes. Heidemann claimed they were the authentic, handwritten personal diaries of Adolf Hitler. This, he explained, was just the beginning. In total, sixty-two volumes existed, a complete personal record written by Führer himself throughout the war.

The potential value of such a find was immeasurable. These volumes were not just military or political documents; they were the purported private thoughts of one of history's most infamous and reviled figures. The appetite for such a discovery was massive. It was a find that promised to rewrite history, offering insights not only to academics and military historians but to an entire world still grappling with the man's legacy. It was, in short, the scoop of the century.

Born in 1938 in Löbau, Saxony, Kujau grew up during the final years of the war and came of age in its aftermath. His family was poor, and like many in East Germany, they lived amid the ruins of a defeated nation. In the years after the war, Nazi memorabilia flooded black markets, and Kujau developed an early fascination with it. By the time he reached adulthood, he had already shown a talent for imitation — first as an artist, then as a forger. He could copy handwriting, mimic paper aging, and create convincing replicas of wartime artifacts. He also had a talent for deception. His early life was marked by small crimes and aliases; he stole food, forged signatures, and spent time in prison for petty theft. When he fled East Germany for the West in the late 1950s, he carried that skill for duplicity with him.

Settling in Stuttgart, Kujau reinvented himself as a businessman and art dealer. By the 1970s, he had built a modest trade selling Nazi-era memorabilia — medals, uniforms, and personal items said to have belonged to prominent officials. His clients were collectors, often nostalgic or obsessed with the war's dark history. Many were gullible, and Kujau quickly learned how easily they could be fooled. He began producing fake Hitler signatures and letters, claiming they came from secret caches hidden by SS officers. His forgeries were so convincing that even experienced collectors were deceived. To maintain the illusion, he cultivated a network of contacts, aliases, and stories. When skeptics questioned his sources, he claimed he was dealing with a high-ranking East German general who possessed Hitler's personal items. Over time, his small operation grew into a lucrative business built entirely on lies.

Around the same time, another man's obsession was taking shape — one that would soon intersect fatally with Kujau's. Gerd Heidemann was a journalist for the German magazine *Stern*, known for his work on historical subjects. Born in Hamburg in 1931, he was too young to have fought in the war but old enough to have been shaped by its aftermath. He collected Nazi memorabilia and even bought Hermann Göring's old yacht, the *Carin II*, which he restored and filled with artifacts. His fascination with the Nazi elite bordered on fixation. By the late 1970s, his career at *Stern* had stagnated. Heidemann needed a story that would restore his reputation — something monumental, something that would make history. When he began hearing rumors about the lost diaries of Adolf Hitler, it felt like destiny.

In 1980, Heidemann learned from a contact in the collectors' world that certain private dealers claimed to possess secret writings by Hitler. The source was mysterious, allegedly linked to an East German officer who had smuggled the materials out of the Soviet zone. Intrigued, Heidemann arranged a meeting. The man who eventually appeared before him was Konrad Kujau, using one of his aliases, "Dr. Fischer." Kujau showed him what he said was one of the recovered notebooks — a small black volume embossed with the initials "A.H." The pages were filled with neat, slanted handwriting in old-style German script. To Heidemann's astonishment, it appeared authentic. Kujau explained that there were many such volumes, each representing a year of Hitler's life. He claimed they had been recovered from the crashed plane near Dresden decades earlier and smuggled to the West through secret channels. This process, he warned, would involve costly and dangerous trips across the border.

The strategy was brilliant. It created a sense of scarcity, danger, and exclusivity, allowing Kujau to produce the forgeries on demand rather than having to create sixty-two volumes upfront. It also allowed him to escalate his price with each new delivery. Heidemann, a trusted and well-respected journalist, took the bait completely. He brought the initial volumes to his editors at *Stern*, who, taking their star reporter at his word, were immediately convinced.

Stern magazine essentially gave Heidemann a blank check. They opened a bank account containing millions of marks, from which Heidemann was authorized to withdraw vast sums of cash to pay Kujau for each new volume. No receipts were required. It was the perfect setup for Heidemann to exploit, so he began skimming off the top, siphoning millions for himself while giving Kujau his cut. On the other hand, Kujau, realizing he had found the biggest sucker in the world, was no longer dealing with small-time collectors but with a major corporation.

The diaries themselves were, by most accounts, banal. They were little more than appointment books filled with mundane observations. Those who read the translations were not confronted with the rants of a sociopath, but with entries about Eva Braun's bad breath or the need to get tickets for the Olympics. But the banality, paradoxically, lent them an air of authenticity. This, the thinking went, is what a real diary would look like — a day-to-day accounting, not a manifesto. The content did not matter; the fact that they were believed to be Hitler's, written in his own hand, was what mattered.

For Heidemann, it was the story of a lifetime. If true, it would be one of the most important historical discoveries since the end of the war. He presented the idea to *Stern's* editors, emphasizing the need for secrecy. The magazine's management, tempted by the potential for global exclusivity, approved initial funds to obtain the materials. The first notebook was purchased for a substantial sum. Handwriting experts hired by *Stern* — though given limited samples for comparison — declared that it could indeed be authentic. The paper looked old, the ink faded appropriately, and the writing style consistent with Hitler's known correspondence. Encouraged, *Stern* continued to buy. Between 1981 and 1983, the magazine paid millions of marks for what eventually became sixty forged volumes — each meticulously produced by Kujau. To protect his cover, he wrote them using fountain pens and old-style paper, soaking the sheets in tea or chemicals to simulate aging. He even manufactured artificial burn marks to suggest the books had survived the plane crash.

As the deal grew, both men were drawn deeper into deception. Kujau enjoyed the money and attention, while Heidemann convinced himself that the diaries were genuine. To others, he repeated the story about the East German source, hinting at secret political connections. The secrecy within *Stern* became extreme. Only a few editors knew the full details, and even they operated under coded references, calling the project "Heiligtum" — "the holy relic." Payments were routed through hidden accounts. The editors dreamed of publishing an exclusive that would elevate *Stern* to global prominence.

In April 1983, after months of negotiation, *Stern* finally decided to go public. A press conference was arranged in Hamburg on April 25. The event drew reporters from around the world. The magazine's editors announced that they had secured Hitler's personal diaries, authenticated by experts, and that the documents would soon be published in serial form. *Stern* sold international rights to major outlets, including *The Sunday Times* in London and *Newsweek* in the United States. The news exploded across headlines. Newspapers described the find as "the greatest historical discovery of the century." Scholars began speculating about what new insights the diaries might reveal into Hitler's mind — his private thoughts, doubts, and daily routines.

At *The Sunday Times*, a senior journalist named Magnus Linklater was tasked with reading the first installment and preparing it for publication. The team was immediately appalled, but not for the reasons one might expect. They were not horrified by the content but bored by it. They had expected world-shaking revelations — why Hitler called off the invasion of England, or his true plans for the Jews. Instead, they found what Linklater called "day-to-day tittle-tattle," with entries complaining about Göring's ill-fitting suits. The material was, by all journalistic standards, terrible.

Furthermore, *Stern's* conditions of sale made proper authentication impossible. Desperate to prevent a leak, they refused to allow anyone from the outside to access the physical diaries. This meant the *Sunday Times* team was kept from the very people and processes that could have exposed the fraud. They were given only facsimiles of some pages and an English translation.

Still, *The Sunday Times* needed some form of authentication to protect its reputation. Murdoch sent Hugh Trevor-Roper, a revered Cambridge historian and a director on News International's board, to validate the purchase. Trevor-Roper was flown to Switzerland, where the diaries were kept in a bank vault. The scene that greeted him was, by design, overwhelming. Dozens of the black, leather-bound volumes were stacked impressively on a table. The sheer scale of the forgery was one of its most convincing elements; no one could believe that a single person would, or could, forge so much.

But the authentication was fatally flawed. Trevor-Roper was the first to admit that his comfort with the German language was limited, and he was completely unfamiliar with the specific Sütterlin script used in Germany in the 1930s and 1940s — a script Kujau was brilliant at forging. Overwhelmed by the spectacle and the pressure, Trevor-Roper made his assessment. When Linklater later called him, desperate for reassurance, the historian said he was 99% convinced they were authentic. For a story of this magnitude, 99% was not good enough.

While Murdoch was negotiating, *Stern* executives, unaware of his internal doubts, were shopping the rights to *Newsweek* in America, asking for $3.6 million. Murdoch, in a brilliant tactical move, called *Newsweek* and suggested they work together on a single, collective bid of half a million dollars. *Newsweek* agreed, and *Stern*, finding its leverage gone, was forced to accept the lowball offer. Murdoch had secured the scoop of the century for a pittance. He had the reassurances of one of the world's leading historians, and that was enough.

In the weeks leading up to publication, Hugh Trevor-Roper began to have serious doubts. He frantically tried to call the paper's editors, stating he was no longer comfortable and wanted to withdraw his backing. When Murdoch was eventually told that his expert now suspected they were fake, his alleged reply was blunt. He went with publication.

On Sunday, April 24, 1983, *The Sunday Times* ran the story with banner headlines, proclaiming the massive exclusive. The issue was a huge success, gaining an extra 60,000 in sales. The editorial team was congratulating itself on one of its greatest front pages when the phone rang. It was Hugh Trevor-Roper. Magnus Linklater and the other editors listened in horror to their editor's side of the conversation. At that moment, the entire foundation for their story collapsed.

The next day, *Stern* magazine held its own triumphant press conference in Hamburg to reveal the source of the diaries to the world. At the press conference, both Trevor-Roper and Weinberg voiced doubts about the authenticity of the Hitler diaries, insisting that German experts must verify them. Trevor-Roper admitted his skepticism stemmed from the lack of evidence linking the books to the 1945 plane crash and lamented that journalistic haste had replaced proper historical verification. *The Guardian* later praised his reversal as an act of "moral courage." Meanwhile, historian David Irving, dismissed by Koch as having "no reputation to lose," challenged the diaries' legitimacy, questioning how Hitler could have written after his arm injury in 1944. Waving photocopied pages, he demanded to know if the ink had been tested — receiving no answer. Chaos erupted as reporters surged forward, and security dragged Irving out as he shouted, "Ink! Ink!"

Suddenly, historians and experts who had been shut out of the process began to point out the obvious. No one in Hitler's surviving inner circle had ever recalled the Führer keeping a diary. Within days, the German Federal Archive (Bundesarchiv) in Berlin was given access to the physical volumes. It did not take them months or years to find the truth; it took a few days. The diaries, they declared, were a laughable and clumsy fake.

The smoking gun was in the material itself. The paper used was from the 1970s. The glue in the bindings was modern, post-war glue. The ink was from a modern pen. The forgery was not clever at all; it was simply audacious. The only reason it had not been exposed immediately was that, in the rush to publish, no one had bothered to conduct the most basic scientific tests.

The most notorious and bizarre mistake, however, was on the cover of each volume. Kujau, attempting to create an official monogram, had embossed the initials "FH" in a fancy German script. He had mistaken the gothic letter "A" for an "F." The initials on the diaries of Adolf Hitler should have been "AH." This simple, glaring error had been missed by Heidemann, by the editors at *Stern*, and by the world-renowned historian Hugh Trevor-Roper.

The scandal that followed was immense. Within weeks, *Stern's* reputation collapsed. The magazine had spent more than nine million marks on the hoax and staked its credibility on it. Public outrage was matched by ridicule. The editors responsible for approving the project were forced to resign. Across Europe and the United States, newspapers that had purchased rights to the diaries faced humiliation.

The subsequent investigation revealed an extraordinary trail of deceit. Police discovered Kujau's workshop filled with pens, inks, papers, and reference books on Hitler's handwriting. He had studied authentic letters in archives and copied phrases from published documents. His imitation was careful but not perfect; he often inserted anachronistic words or repeated phrases that Hitler never used. Kujau admitted that he had forged every volume himself. Heidemann, however, insisted that he too had been deceived — that he had believed the diaries to be genuine and had merely acted as an intermediary. Prosecutors disagreed. Evidence showed that Heidemann had siphoned off large sums of the money *Stern* provided for purchases, claiming the funds were needed for secret payments to East German couriers. In reality, much of it had gone to his personal accounts, spent on luxuries and debts.

The trial began in August 1984 in Hamburg. It was a spectacle. Reporters filled the courtroom, eager for details about how one of Europe's most respected magazines had been fooled. Kujau, dressed neatly and sometimes smiling for the cameras, seemed to enjoy the attention. He admitted his guilt readily and even demonstrated his forgery techniques for the court. Heidemann maintained that he had acted in good faith, though his credibility was destroyed by the financial evidence. In July 1985, the verdict was delivered. Kujau was sentenced to four and a half years in prison; Heidemann to four years and eight months. The sentences were surprisingly light, with the judge noting that the "stupidity" and negligence of the *Stern* management meant they had to share in the culpability. Both served about half their terms before being released. *Stern's* editors who had approved the project were dismissed from their positions, and the magazine's reputation never fully recovered.

After his release, Kujau briefly became a minor celebrity. He appeared on talk shows, opened a small art gallery, and even sold authorized "Kujau copies" of famous paintings — this time openly labeling them as reproductions. He seemed to revel in the absurdity of his fame, often mocking the very people who had once been deceived. Heidemann, by contrast, withdrew from public life, embittered and financially ruined. The "Hitler Diaries" episode haunted him for the rest of his life.

The legacy of the hoax was uneven. Hugh Trevor-Roper's career was destroyed; the historian never recovered from the public humiliation. Gerd Heidemann was left ruined, professionally and financially. Konrad Kujau died in Stuttgart in 2000, but not before his book, detailing his life of crime, earned him the millions the diaries never had.

And Rupert Murdoch? *The Sunday Times*, like *Stern*, had to print a massive retraction. But in the media world, scandal sells. After the initial "Hitler Diaries" exclusive, the paper sold just as many copies, if not more, with the follow-up headline: "The Hitler Diaries Hoax." Murdoch's paper reportedly retained 20,000 of the new readers they had gained from the debacle. For him, it didn't matter if the story was fake, because he was still making money. The hoax was a disaster for journalism, but for a press baron, it was just another profitable news cycle.

17

THE CARTEL HUNTER

In a small diner, three people sat at a table, existing in separate worlds. On one side sat Miriam Rodriguez, a middle-aged mother, her back straight, staring at the two young men opposite her as if in a tense business meeting. The man directly across from her, Sama, was focused on her, but his attention was constantly split by the walkie-talkie buzzing on the table. Through its static, Miriam could hear voices calling out street names, tracking police and military patrols in the area. It was the only reason she knew his name. The third man, oblivious to the tension, was scarfing down his food like it was his last meal. When he finished, he eyed Miriam's untouched sandwich. "You going to eat that?" he asked. She pushed the plate toward him.

Sama leaned forward. "Your daughter smoke weed or something?" Miriam was taken aback. "Excuse me?" He explained that her daughter, Karen, was surprisingly relaxed for a kidnap victim, super chill. He said he liked that, and it made him want to let her go. Miriam knew she had to play along, but a cold certainty had already settled in her heart. Her daughter had been taken by the Zetas, one of the most dangerous cartels in Mexico. No one got out alive.

Sama told her the decision wasn't his, but for $2,000, he could try to convince the big boss to spare her. Miriam smiled, a hollow gesture. She knew these men, the ones sitting in front of her eating her food, had already killed her daughter. And in that moment, she knew she would not stop until every single one of them paid for it.

The Zetas were not always a cartel. They began as Hired Guns, an elite paramilitary wing of the Gulf Cartel, one of Mexico's oldest and most powerful criminal syndicates. The original Zetas were former members of the Mexican Army's elite Special Forces, many of whom had received extensive training in urban warfare, sniper tactics, and explosives from the United States military, ironically to fight the cartels. The leader of the Gulf Cartel recruited thirty of these agents to be his personal bodyguards, offering them pay the government could never match. This private army was lethally effective, but soon, they realized their strength. If they were the part that made the Gulf Cartel so special, why did they need the Gulf Cartel?

The Zetas split off and declared war on their former employers on March 31, 2010. The battle for control of the northeastern border, a prime smuggling route, began in Miriam's hometown of San Fernando. In the early morning hours, the Zetas staged a fake highway accident to lure police and firefighters to an isolated road. Once the authorities were gathered, a convoy of makeshift tanks — modified trucks, SUVs, and even a school bus, all spray-painted with the letter "Z" and outfitted with gun mounts — appeared on the highway. For six hours, from 4:00 a.m. to 10:00 a.m., they drove block by block, firing into every public building, riddling police stations and courthouses with bullets. The message was clear: the Gulf Cartel was no longer in charge.

The Gulf Cartel fought back, plunging San Fernando into a full-scale war. Civilians became collateral damage in a conflict that saw tens of thousands of innocent people die. The Zetas' initial, surgical violence soon gave way to a new philosophy. As they ran out of elite Special Forces to recruit, they began forcing younger, more volatile, and more sadistic members into their ranks. To keep them loyal, Zeta leadership gave these new cells a free-for-all: they could earn their own money through any means necessary — extortion, theft, human trafficking — as long as they did not interfere with the cartel's primary business of drug and oil smuggling.

This policy unleashed a new kind of terror. The Zetas, who had once left civilians alone, now targeted them. They weren't just violent; they were theatrical in their cruelty, specializing in torture, decapitation, and dissolving bodies in acid, a practice they called "cooking." They posted their executions online. They ruled not just through power but through psychological warfare. They were accused of not following the "gentleman's code" of other cartels, killing pregnant women and dismembering victims alive in front of their families.

In this atmosphere of fear lived Miriam Rodríguez. Born and raised in Tamaulipas, she was known for her stubbornness and her courage. She had survived cancer, built a small business selling cowboy hats, and raised her children with discipline and warmth. Her home in San Fernando sat near the main road leading to the U.S. border, a route that traffickers and migrants shared in uneasy proximity. Like many parents in her region, she tried to shield her children from the danger that had become part of everyday life. Her daughter, Karen, was twenty when she disappeared.

On January 24, 2014, while working as a nanny in Texas, Miriam received a call at 4:00 a.m. from her eldest daughter, Azalea, who was crying and said something terrible had happened to Karen. By 8:00 a.m., Miriam was already on a bus heading back to San Fernando. Azalea told her what had taken place that night: their estranged father, Luis, had come to her door unexpectedly in the middle of the night. As he stepped inside, his phone rang, and a man on the other end told him they had his daughter and demanded a ransom of $77,000 for her release. Moments later, Karen's voice came through the line, pleading for him to pay, saying that if he didn't, this might be the last time they would hear from her.

The demand was impossible. The average annual salary in Mexico was around $15,000. They had until 3:00 p.m. the next day. By 10:00 a.m., the family had pooled their entire life savings and secured a business loan, amounting to less than $10,000. Luis went to drop the money off at a local health center while Miriam watched from a distance. A skinny teenage boy grabbed the bag and told Luis to meet him at the cemetery in twenty minutes to retrieve Karen. The boy jumped into a cherry-red Ford Explorer and sped off. At the cemetery, the family waited, but Karen never arrived.

The next day, the kidnappers called, claiming the rainstorm had prevented the exchange. Then, they broke into Miriam's house, where Karen lived, and stole some of her things. They called back and demanded more money. Miriam borrowed another $2,000 from everyone she could think of and paid it. It was everything they had. But Karen never came home.

For a month Miriam sank into a deep depression; the kidnapping had shattered everything she believed. She had taught her children that keeping their heads down and staying out of trouble would keep the cartels away, an unspoken bargain that now felt broken. The Zetas were no longer striking only the wealthy or their enemies — they were preying on anyone. On February 23, 2014, one month after Karen's abduction, Miriam rose, put on a full face of makeup for the first time in weeks, and went downstairs. She told Azalea that she no longer expected Karen to be returned, that she believed her daughter was dead, and that for the rest of her life she would hunt down the people responsible and make them pay.

Her investigation began almost accidentally. She started visiting the places Karen had gone before her abduction, talking to shopkeepers, taxi drivers, and anyone who might remember seeing her that day. Bit by bit, she began assembling fragments of the story. The kidnappers were part of a local Zeta cell, led by men who had once been neighbors, men she might have passed on the street. With every piece of information, Miriam grew bolder. She followed clues that the police ignored, calling phone numbers, comparing handwriting on ransom notes, and noting the details of cars and houses. But the real break came from Carlos, a friend of Karen's who had also been kidnapped that night but was later released. For months, Carlos was terrified to speak, but he eventually told Miriam what happened.

Carlos had gone to Karen's house to fix her car. When he arrived, two men came out of the house and invited him in to wait for her. Inside, he found Karen on the floor, her hands and feet bound, her face bloody and swollen. The men tied up Carlos and his cousin and proceeded to beat Karen, accusing her of working for the Gulf Cartel. She screamed that they had the wrong person, but they didn't listen, torturing her and suffocating her with a plastic bag.

The group was moved to a Zeta ranch, where they were lined up with other captives. A female Zeta member, seemingly enraged by Karen's appearance, grabbed her by the hair, straddled her back, and smashed her head against the floor, screaming, "This is for being so pretty!" The captives were forced to call their families for ransom. The next morning, the men were loaded into a truck. The two women, Karen and her friend Barbara, were dragged to a tree. Carlos saw the men tying a yellow rope around their necks, flinging it over a branch, and start beating them with sticks as if they were piñatas.

With this information, Miriam had a new target: the boy who had collected the ransom money. He was known as "the Florist." Miriam knew him; as a child, he was one of the hungry neighborhood kids she would often feed. He had later tried to give Karen flowers, which she always politely declined. Miriam tracked him down, tackled him, jammed her loaded pistol into his back, and whispered, "If you move, I will shoot you." He was her eleventh target.

Miriam's hunt was methodical and relentless. She was a master of disguise, changing her appearance, cutting her hair, and adopting different personas to get close to her targets. She tracked down one of the kidnappers, a young man named Cristiano, who had just turned eighteen. He had been the second man at the diner, the one who ate her sandwich. He was arrested and confessed, giving Miriam more names. During his interrogation, the boy kept asking for his mom and complaining that he was hungry. Miriam, watching from another room, walked in and handed him her own lunch. She later told the baffled police, "He's a child. No matter what he did, when I heard him saying he was hungry, it was like I heard my own child."

Her hunt became something of a running joke in the family: Miriam had always wanted to be a cop, but she wasn't corrupt enough to qualify. Fearless by nature, she had already confronted the Zetas once before. Years earlier, her son-in-law, Ernesto, had received a letter detailing his every move, followed by a phone number and a demand for ransom to prevent his kidnapping. Miriam took control of the negotiations, snapping at the Zeta on the phone that they didn't have that kind of money and calling him an idiot. She insisted on handling the drop-off herself. When

Azalea tried to stop her, Miriam revealed a pistol tucked in her jacket, questioning what the criminals could want with an old woman like her, and instructing her daughter that if she wasn't back in fifteen minutes, she should pack up, take Karen, and flee to the U.S. At the abandoned gas station, Miriam tossed the bag of cash out the window and drove away, refusing to get out of the car.

This tenacity had always defined Miriam. When she was diagnosed with cancer while Karen was just four, she told the doctors that she couldn't die — there was a young child depending on her, and no one else would take care of her. She beat the cancer. Later, when her doctors warned that her weight posed a serious health risk, she underwent gastric bypass surgery, a procedure that would also help her in her quest. She spent her days hiking through abandoned ranches and staking out safe houses, relentlessly pursuing those responsible.

Miriam also turned her fight into activism, founding the "Vanishing Collective" to support other families of the disappeared. She taught them how to navigate the system, demand compensation, and pressure the government, becoming notorious for confronting and threatening officials while showing families that they had power in numbers. Through her relentless detective work, she brought Karen's killers to justice. She tracked down El Flo, who had left the cartel and was working in a factory, and found El Kike, the man alleged to have pulled the rope, arranging for his arrest at church. When the minister asked if she had mercy, Miriam met his gaze and asked where El Kike's mercy had been when he killed her daughter.

Her children begged her to stop. Authorities had recovered a few of Karen's rib bones from the ranch — just enough for a burial — but Miriam was far from finished. At the burial she opened the coffin, removed the small bag of bones, and held it aloft, telling those gathered that this was all she had left of her daughter and that she had no intention of stopping now.

In March 2017, three years after Karen's murder, twenty-nine inmates, many of them Zetas Miriam had put away, tunneled their way out of prison. For the first time, Miriam was terrified. She knew they would come for her. The police, who were legally required to protect her, offered no help. Her friends and family tried to reassure her, arguing that the Zetas were weakened and wouldn't be foolish enough to kill a high-profile national advocate like her. It would bring too much heat from the government. But Miriam knew better. "I can only hope," she told her children, "if those bastards come after me, they give me a chance to shoot back."

On May 10, 2017 — Mother's Day in Mexico — Azalea was waiting for her mother to meet her for coffee and cake. The call came from her father instead. Miriam had been getting out of her car in front of her ex-husband's house when a car drove by and fired thirteen rounds. She was hit eight times. Her son, Luis, found her with her hand in her purse, reaching for the pistol she always carried. She was pronounced dead at the hospital.

Miriam's death did not end her quest. Luis, who had never wanted to be part of her fight, found himself inheriting it. He took over the collective, and at his mother's funeral, a childhood friend gave him a tip, a name: "El Luche." Luis learned that the Zetas who escaped had not come for her themselves; they had hired a separate cell to kill her because she was causing them too much trouble. Luis, becoming more like his mother every day, began his own hunt. He helped authorities track down El Luche, who was killed before he could be arrested, and the other members of the hit squad. And finally, Luis found the last person on his mother's list: the woman who had beaten Karen for being pretty. He had her arrested.

Unlike his mother, Luis decided to stop. He had avenged his sister and his mother, but he wanted to protect what was left of his family. He now focuses on helping other victims' families through the collective his mother built, ending the cycle of vengeance that had consumed his mother and, for a time, himself.

18

"JESUS WAS AN ALIEN"

In the 1980s, a wave of fear known as the "Satanic Panic" swept across North America and parts of Europe, fueled by media reports and public anxiety about alleged ritual abuse, black magic, and the influence of dangerous cults. This moral panic, often amplified by evangelical Christian communities wary of rising occultism and alternative spiritualities, created an environment where suspicion and accusation could easily take root. While the panic was most prominent in the United States, its echoes reached far corners of the globe, including the remote towns nestled deep within the Brazilian Amazon. It was in this atmosphere of heightened fear and fascination with the dark side of spirituality that a small, obscure group known as the Superior Universal Alignment, led by a charismatic woman named Valentina de Andrade, would become entangled in one of the most horrific and disturbing series of crimes in Brazil's history.

Valentina de Andrade was born in the city of Carazinho in southern Brazil on September 28, 1931. Little is known about her early life beyond what she chose to reveal in her later biographical writings. She described a modest upbringing in a small town, lacking toys or bicycles, and claimed to be semi-illiterate, suggesting she intentionally avoided formal education to preserve her "authenticity." She portrayed herself as a romantic, an extrovert, loyal, affectionate, and possessing "unquestionable dignity." Crucially, she claimed never to have "practiced a single act of evilness." This self-constructed image of purity and innate wisdom laid the groundwork for her later claims to spiritual authority.

In 1981, at the age of fifty, Valentina experienced what she described as a life-altering spiritual awakening. She claimed to have been contacted by divine cosmic beings, extraterrestrials who delivered visions warning her of an impending doomsday. These beings, she asserted, promised to save her and her followers aboard a spaceship if she spread their message. This became the foundation of her belief system: she was a "materialized energy," a "cosmic entity of light, love, and truth," receiving divine knowledge from beyond Earth. Her teachings incorporated a wide array of esoteric concepts — reincarnation, recovering memories from past lives, energy fields, ghosts, life after death — alongside a central, controversial claim: Jesus was not God, but an extraterrestrial, and the traditional concept of God was a "big farce."

Valentina settled in the town of Altamira, located in the state of Pará deep within the Amazon region. There, her neighbors began to perceive her as having clairvoyant abilities. She became the local seer and fortune teller, charging people for insights into their future. Her popularity grew, especially after she published a book outlining her core beliefs, including the extraterrestrial nature of Jesus. Capitalizing on this local fame, she officially founded her group, the Superior Universal Alignment, in 1981.

Like many cult leaders promising salvation from apocalypse, Valentina claimed to know the exact date the world would end, a secret she shared only with her most devoted followers. A core tenet of her burgeoning cult was particularly disturbing: she declared that any child born after 1981 was a reincarnation of evil and needed to be "expunged." Prospective members with children were forced to abandon them, either giving them to family members or putting them up for adoption, as these children, deemed "unconscious instruments of the great scam called God," would not be allowed on the rescue spacecraft.

As Valentina cultivated her following, the inevitable happened: her prophesied doomsday dates came and went without incident. Rather than questioning her authority, however, her followers internalized the failure.

Manipulated by Valentina, they came to believe the spaceship hadn't arrived because *their* faith was insufficient, because *they* had not proven their loyalty. This dynamic deepened their dependence on her, reinforcing her control.

It was around 1989, amidst this environment of unwavering belief and Valentina's increasingly hostile stance toward children born after 1981, that a terrifying pattern began to emerge in Altamira. Young boys, primarily between the ages of eight and fourteen, started disappearing. Many came from impoverished families; some were orphans or homeless, scraping by shining shoes or doing odd jobs. The horror began not with death but with brutal assault.

On August 2, 1989, an eight-year-old boy named José was lured away by a strange man. Hours later, he was found alive but severely injured and showing signs of sexual abuse. Then, on November 16, ten-year-old Otoniel was invited by a man to share some mangoes he had just delivered. The man led him to an isolated area, incapacitated him with a chemical-soaked cloth, and when Otoniel awoke, he discovered he had been sexually abused and castrated. He survived but endured years of psychological trauma and dozens of painful, ultimately unsuccessful reconstructive surgeries. On July 23, 1990, nine-year-old Walda Clay encountered a man near the edge of town who asked for help getting a kite out of a tree. Lured into the woods, he too was rendered unconscious, sexually abused, and castrated. Like Otoniel, he faced a long road of surgeries and psychological recovery.

These initial survivors offered the first terrifying glimpses of the attacker, or attackers. They described a single man acting alone, using chemical cloths to subdue them before inflicting horrific mutilations. But soon, the attacks escalated from assault to murder. Between 1989 and 1993, nineteen boys disappeared in and around Altamira. As the bodies began to be found, a sickening pattern became undeniable.

The list of victims grew steadily, each discovery more horrifying than the last. Tito Mendes, thirteen, vanished on January 20, 1991, last seen with an unknown man near a stream. He was never found. Elton Fonseca, ten, went missing on May 5, 1991; his mutilated remains were found forty-six days later, only to mysteriously disappear from the morgue before an autopsy could be performed. Eleven-year-old J.C.B. disappeared in August 1991. On New Year's Day 1992, thirteen-year-old Judirley da Cunha's body was found days after he vanished; he was naked, castrated, sexually assaulted, and bore severe burn wounds. Ednaldo de Souza Teixeira, twelve, was found beaten to death beside a well in April 1992. Jaques de Silva Pessoã, thirteen, disappeared while tending cattle in October 1992; his body was found castrated, abused, tortured, with his eyes gouged out and hands chopped off. Clebson Varrêra Caĺdus, thirteen, was found murdered in November 1992, naked, castrated, and tortured. Fabrício Férris de Souza, twelve, vanished in December 1992 after being seen with a man on a red bicycle. The horror continued into 1993: Raylan Santos de Souza, nine, disappeared in January after being seen with two men near the Xingu River. Flávio Lopes de Silva, ten, went missing in March; his body was found tortured, his genitals mutilated, and covered in strange circular wounds later identified as human bite marks, suggesting possible cannibalism. R.F.S., an eleven-year-old shoeshiner, vanished in July 1993.

The community was gripped by terror. The local police, led by Chief Éder Mauro, struggled to connect the cases. Initial investigations were hampered by lack of evidence and, potentially, indifference toward the victims, most of whom came from poor backgrounds. An early suspect, a local drifter named Rotílio de Souza, was arrested but died suspiciously in custody only months later. When the disappearances continued, police had to admit he wasn't the sole perpetrator, if involved at all.

As the body count rose, investigators noted the precise, almost surgical nature of some mutilations, particularly the castration and the potential removal of internal organs in some cases. This led to a theory that the boys were being kidnapped for an organ trafficking ring. Suspicion fell on two doctors who had recently moved to Altamira, Anísio Ferreira de Souza and Césio Flávio Caldas Brandão. They were detained for questioning, but experts pointed out that the violent manner in which the bodies were mutilated would likely have rendered any organs unusable for transplant. With no evidence, the doctors were released.

The investigation stalled until one boy managed to escape his captors and identify them. His testimony implicated several high-ranking members of the Altamira community: a police officer, the two doctors previously suspected, the son of a wealthy land baron, and, crucially, Valentina de Andrade, the leader of the Superior Universal Alignment. Suddenly, the small, secretive cult was thrust into the center of the investigation.

Rumors, fueled by the ongoing Satanic Panic and Valentina's own anti-child rhetoric, began to spread like wildfire. Tales of ritualistic abuse, black magic, and cannibalism associated with the cult gripped the community and the media. Police, perhaps eager for a simple explanation or influenced by the prevailing panic, leaned heavily into the cult angle. They searched Valentina's estate, finding ritualistic hoods and videotapes of ceremonies. On one tape, police claimed Valentina entered a trance and ordered her followers to "kill little children." However, linguistic experts later reviewed the poor-quality audio and concluded she more likely said, "Yes, there are more experienced little children." The tape was deemed inadmissible.

Valentina maintained her innocence, claiming she hadn't even been in Altamira since 1987, years before the murders began. Despite the lack of physical evidence connecting her or the cult to the crimes, Chief Mauro seemed determined to pin the blame on them, publicly promoting the theory that the murders were committed during satanic rituals.

Parallel to the Altamira investigation, a similar horror unfolded miles away. On April 6, 1992, six-year-old Evandro Ramos Caetano went missing in Guaratuba, Paraná. Five days later, his mutilated body was found. His hair, toes, ears, genitals, and hands had been cut off, and his intestines, liver, and heart were missing. Investigators, echoing the Altamira theories, suspected human sacrifice. They accused Celina Abbage, the wife of the town's former mayor, and her daughter Beatriz, of paying cult members $2,000 to kill the boy as part of a black magic ritual to revive her husband's failing political career. Police claimed the women confessed, but they later retracted, alleging torture. Despite the lack of autopsy, forensic examination, or physical evidence, Celina and Beatriz spent nearly six years in prison before being acquitted in 1998. Beatriz was fully pardoned in 2016. This case, dubbed "The Witches of Guaratuba," highlighted the authorities' willingness to pursue ritualistic theories even in the absence of proof.

Back in Altamira, the case against the Superior Universal Alignment members continued, built almost entirely on questionable eyewitness testimony and coerced confessions. One key witness, Edmilson da Silva Frazão, claimed to have attended a ritual at Dr. Souza's house in 1991 where he saw Valentina. However, his testimony was inconsistent; he couldn't recall the date, initially saying 1989 or 1990, contradicting his earlier police statement which cited 1991. Despite these inconsistencies, the judge allowed his testimony.

Other former cult members testified, denying any ritualistic crimes but confirming Valentina's requirement that members abandon children born after 1981. They portrayed her as coercive but stopped short of accusing her of murder. Two of the surviving victims, Otoniel and another unnamed boy, identified one man as their attacker: Carlos Alberto Santos Lima, a military police officer who worked as a security guard for Amaílton Madeira Gomes, the son of the wealthy land baron, who was also implicated.

Despite the focus solely on Carlos Alberto by the victims, the prosecution pressed forward against all the indicted individuals connected to the cult. The investigation was riddled with flaws: no autopsies, no crime scene forensics, retracted confessions due to alleged police torture, and conflicting eyewitness accounts. The chief prosecutor himself argued for dismissal due to lack of evidence, but an assistant prosecutor pushed forward, and a judge ultimately pronounced the accused guilty in 1994.

The convictions were immediately appealed. A new prosecutor reviewed the case and accepted the appeal, citing the profound lack of evidence. This decision sparked public outrage, with protests erupting in Belém. Fearing for his life, the prosecutor fled Altamira. However, the courts eventually ordered a new hearing and nullified the convictions due to the investigation's egregious flaws. Dr. Brandão, after spending over two years in prison without trial, sued the state, claiming he was used as a scapegoat. All other defendants connected to the cult were released in 1995.

Valentina de Andrade, having had her name cleared early on and possessing an alibi placing her out of the country during the murders, had already fled Brazil. She moved to Argentina, continuing her cult activities with a diminished following, steadfastly maintaining her innocence regarding the Altamira horrors. Her current whereabouts, and whether she is still alive, remain unknown.

With the cult theory dismantled, the question remained: who killed the children of Altamira? The answer may lie with Francisco das Chagas Rodrigues de Brito. Born in 1965, Francisco endured a childhood of abandonment and abuse. He eventually settled in Altamira in the 1980s, working as a bicycle mechanic, precisely when the murders began. He fit the profile: a local man who could easily gain the trust of young boys working on the streets.

Francisco left Altamira and continued his horrific spree across Brazil, moving from city to city. His methods remained consistent: luring poor young boys, raping them, mutilating their genitals, ears, and fingers, and then killing them, often by strangulation or stabbing, sometimes burning their bodies. His victims were always boys, typically aged between four and fifteen.

He was finally caught in 2004 after the murder of fifteen-year-old Jonathan Viegas, who had told someone he was going to meet a bicycle mechanic just before disappearing. Police arrested Francisco, and a search of his home uncovered bones and clothing belonging to two victims. They found cut T-shirts matching those worn by other victims and realized his victims were always found within 600 feet (about 182 meters) of where he lived. Investigators connected him to the deaths of young boys dating back to 1989, spanning his time in Altamira. He was ultimately suspected of killing and mutilating up to forty-two boys across Brazil.

Francisco confessed to murdering seventeen boys but refused to provide details. Due to the botched initial investigations and lack of preserved physical evidence from the Altamira crime scenes years earlier, police could not definitively link him to those specific murders, even though his timeline and methods matched perfectly. The case against the cult had muddied the waters irrevocably. Francisco das Chagas Rodrigues de Brito was convicted for the murders he confessed to and sentenced to 580 years in prison, recognized as one of Brazil's most prolific serial killers.

The truth of what happened in Altamira remains obscured by incompetence, corruption, and the lingering shadow of the Satanic Panic.

While Francisco das Chagas appears to be the most likely perpetrator, the possibility of accomplices, or even a separate group operating concurrently, cannot be entirely dismissed. The sloppy police work and the rush to blame an unconventional religious group allowed a monster to continue killing for years. For the families of the victims, the lack of definitive answers and the system's failures represent a profound and enduring injustice.

19

THE WOMAN IN THE VALLEY OF DEATH

To an outsider, Isdalen, or the "Ice Valley," might seem an unusual place for a stroll. It's a desolate but starkly beautiful valley east of Bergen, Norway, where a large, dark lake fills the basin and pine forests climb the hillsides until they give way to barren rock and boulders. Its reputation is as treacherous as its terrain; another of its nicknames is the "Valley of Death," a nod to the many hiking accidents that have occurred on its hazardous trails and a darker, more ancient rumor that it was once a site where people in medieval times would walk to end their lives. November is a particularly cold and wet time of year in this part of the world, with only a few precious hours of sunlight each day. But on the morning of November 29, 1970, a university professor, familiar with the valley's paths, was out for a hike with his two young daughters, aged ten and twelve. They could not have imagined that their familiar walk was about to lead them to the heart of one of Norway's most profound and enduring mysteries.

As they navigated the trail, one of the girls spotted something unusual sticking out from behind a cluster of boulders. From a distance, her father thought it looked like a human foot, and his immediate concern was that a hiker had been injured. He hurried his children toward the spot, but as they drew closer, a repugnant and unsettling smell hit them — the unmistakable stench of burnt flesh hanging heavy in the crisp morning air. When they rounded the final boulder, the scene that confronted them was one of absolute horror. There was indeed a person there, a woman, but she was beyond any help. The professor quickly shielded his daughters' eyes, turned them around, and marched them out of the treacherous valley as quickly as he could to find a phone and call the police.

A small team of officers was dispatched to Isdalen, and they, too, were met with the same nauseating smell of burning as they approached the location. The woman lay on her back between the rocks, her body contorted into a disturbing posture known as a "boxer pose," with her fists clenched and her limbs flexed — a common, gruesome result of the dehydration and shrinkage of muscles in bodies exposed to intense heat. The entire front of her body was horrifically burned, the skin and clothing charred away, yet strangely, her back was completely untouched by the fire. There was no sign of a campfire or any other source for the blaze that had consumed her.

Scattered around her were a peculiar collection of belongings: a pair of rubber boots, two plastic water bottles that were partially melted, a purse, an umbrella, some jewelry, and a watch that was stopped, as if for display, at 10:10. Underneath her body, investigators found a fur hat that, when tested, revealed traces of petrol. This was the only hint of an accelerant, but there was no canister to be found. Even more bizarre was a deliberate and systematic effort to erase her identity. All the labels on her belongings had been meticulously removed or rubbed off, and every single tag on her clothing had been carefully cut away. This was no accident. The scene was immediately treated as a potential murder, but with a victim who was seemingly a ghost, burnt beyond easy recognition and stripped of any identifying marks, the police had no leads.

The woman's body was sent to a local university hospital for an autopsy, which only deepened the enigma. While the fire had clearly been a factor in her death — she had soot in her respiratory tract and signs of carbon monoxide poisoning — the toxicology report revealed another shocking detail. Her system was flooded with barbiturates. It was estimated she had ingested between fifty and seventy sleeping pills, a brand known to be sold in England and tragically popular among women who intended to commit suicide by overdose. Some of the pills were found undigested in her stomach, and according to one source, a few were still in her mouth when she died.

This finding threw the investigation into confusion. Was this a murder or a suicide? The sheer number of pills pointed toward a self-inflicted act, but the rest of the scene made little sense. Why would someone travel to such a remote and unusual location, consume a massive overdose of sleeping pills, and then set themselves on fire with petrol, all without leaving the container behind? The questions were piling up, with no answers in sight.

Three days later, the police got their first real break. A call came in from the luggage storage office at the Bergen train station. A week prior, on November 23rd, someone had checked in two suitcases and had never returned to collect them. When investigators opened the suitcases, the mystery of the Isdal Woman suddenly took on a life of its own. Inside, they found a fingerprint on a pair of non-prescription eyeglasses that matched the victim, confirming the luggage was hers. The contents revealed a woman who was well-traveled and meticulously prepared, yet fanatically secretive. The suitcases held wigs, fancy clothing, coats, cosmetics, and an eczema cream. But just as with the items at the death scene, every single label on her clothes and personal effects had been painstakingly removed or rubbed off.

There were, however, a few items that provided clues. They found 500 German Deutschmarks, a sewing kit from a hotel in Geneva, a spoon with the letters 'SCHP' engraved on it that was traced to an Austrian manufacturer, and a matchbook from a German erotic underwear company. Most importantly, they discovered a notebook that contained what at first appeared to be a sophisticated code — lines of numbers and letters. But the detail that would kick off the manhunt in earnest was a simple shopping bag from a shoe store in the city of Stavanger, south of Bergen.

Following this lead, investigators traveled to the shoe shop, where the owner vividly remembered the woman. He recalled serving her on November 18th, noting that she stood out. She was good-looking, he said, and spoke English with an accent he couldn't quite place. Another worker described her as being around five foot seven (about 1.67 meters) tall with dark hair, brown eyes, and a well-put-together appearance that seemed at odds with what the shopkeeper described as an unpleasant, garlic-like smell — something uncommon in Norway at the time. As he went to the basement to get her size, she called out to him in another language he thought might be German or French. The police now had a strong sense she was not from the area, so they began checking hotels in Stavanger.

They quickly found one right by the shoe shop. Staff there confirmed she had stayed for nine days, from November 9th to the 18th, in a small room without a bathroom. The bellboy remembered her, noting her heavy makeup and serious, rarely smiling demeanor. It was unusual for a lone woman to stay at the hotel for so long, especially in November, which was not a tourist season. When asked where she was from, she had told him Belgium. According to the hotel registration card she filled out, her name was Finella Lorck, and she was from Belgium. But when authorities checked, they found that no such person existed, and the passport number she had provided was a fake.

The Isdal Woman was a phantom, and her trail was a labyrinth of lies. The case had now attracted international attention, and Norway's secret police became involved — an unusual step for what was, on the surface, a local murder investigation. The mysterious notebook was sent to a military codebreaker, who soon realized it wasn't a sophisticated cipher at all, but rather a personal shorthand. Each line of letters and numbers represented a place and a date, documenting her extensive travels. Soon, police had a stack of hotel registration cards from all over Norway and even from other countries like France, all filled out in the same distinctive handwriting but all bearing different names and different Belgian birthplaces. The cards were mostly written in German, but with peculiar spelling errors and phrasing that suggested it was not her first language. She was juggling at least eight different fake identities, each with its own corresponding fake passport.

One hotel card, from the very last hotel she stayed in before she died, showed a distinct change in her penmanship. Handwriting experts confirmed it was the same person, but concluded that she had been deliberately trying to disguise her writing. This raised a chilling question: in her final days, was the Isdal Woman trying to hide from someone? The codebreaker was able to decipher all but the final line in her notebook: "M L 23 N M M." It was clear that "23 N" represented November 23rd, the day she checked her luggage at the station and was last seen alive, but the meaning of the initials "ML" and "MM" remains unknown to this day.

As investigators pieced together her movements, witness accounts began to emerge that placed her in the company of several unidentified men — details that were strangely absent from the official police reports. During a stay at the Hotel Neptune in Bergen in early November, a waitress remembered seeing her sitting alone one evening, looking sad. The following night, however, she was in the restaurant again, this time with an older, gray-haired man who the waitress believed might be Norwegian. The encounter was unsettlingly silent. The man read from a sheet of paper while the Isdal Woman sat stiffly, a serious look on her face, not saying a single word. The waitress was adamant that it felt like a serious meeting, not a romantic date.

Just a few days before her death, on the night of November 18th, after arriving in Bergen from Stavanger, she checked into the Hotel Rosenkrantz. That evening, a maid, believing the room to be empty, knocked briefly before entering to turn down the bed. She was startled to find the Isdal Woman lying in bed and, sitting in a chair across the room, a young man with blonde hair wearing a gray suit. The maid apologized and quickly made the bed while the pair watched her in complete, unnerving silence. Neither of them said a word. Again, this encounter with an unknown man was seemingly ignored in the police investigation, and neither of these men ever came forward after her death became public knowledge.

The next morning, she checked out and moved a short distance to the Hotel Hordenheimen — the hotel where she disguised her handwriting on the registration card. Her behavior there continued to be bizarre. She took a corner room, giving her a perfect view of both streets leading up to the hotel. Housekeepers noted that the "do not disturb" sign was almost always on her door, and when she wasn't in the room, she had a strange habit of moving an armchair from her room out into the hallway, only to bring it back inside when she returned. On November 23rd, she checked out, took a taxi to the train station, left her suitcases in a locker, and vanished until her burnt body was discovered a week later in the Valley of Death.

The involvement of the secret police, the systematic erasure of her identity, and her extensive, well-funded travels all pointed toward one tantalizing conclusion: the Isdal Woman was a spy. This theory gained significant weight when a critical witness account finally came to light years later. A fisherman from a small port near Stavanger claimed to have seen her on the docks speaking for a long time with a naval officer aboard a military vessel. The fisherman reported this to the police, but it's unclear if he was ever formally interviewed before the case was abruptly closed.

What happened next, however, was even stranger. Just before Christmas, as the fisherman and his family were about to board a train for a holiday in London, two men in plain clothes approached him on the platform, identified themselves as police, and took him aside for a twenty-minute conversation. He later revealed to his family that the men — who never showed any ID — had handed him a small handgun and a knife, telling him to keep them on him at all times in London in case he needed to protect himself. He was left terrified, with no idea who he was supposed to be protecting himself from. This felt less like a police interview and more like a thinly veiled threat to ensure his silence.

The reason a naval ship was in the docks that day was critical. The Norwegian Navy was conducting top-secret tests of the new Penguin missile system, a cutting-edge piece of Cold War technology that could be launched from small ships and was of immense interest to the Soviet Union. Norway was a founding member of the North Atlantic Treaty Organization (NATO), and Russia was known to be closely monitoring its highly developed arms industry, with Russian ships often spotted near the test zones. The Isdal Woman's travels between Stavanger and Bergen seemed to coincide perfectly with numerous tests of the missile system, and she had even been spotted near the test sites on more than one occasion.

It all seemed to add up, but if she was a spy, she was a clumsy one. Experts in espionage point out that she stood out everywhere she went, a fatal flaw for an undercover agent. A professional spy would have one or two solid, well-researched false identities, not a chaotic tangle of eight or more, and wouldn't need to cut the labels from their clothing. It's possible she wasn't a spy in the traditional sense, but perhaps an information courier, moving between operatives to pass along intelligence, which could explain her silent meetings with the various men.

Despite the compelling espionage theories, the Bergen police officially closed the investigation after only three weeks, declaring her death a tragic suicide. The decision was met with frustration from both the press and the police officers on the case, who felt that their hands had been tied by the secret police and that promising leads abroad were never pursued. In a final, somber act, the police themselves held a funeral for the unknown woman. In a small Bergen graveyard, sixteen men and two women from the force watched as a white, zinc-lined coffin — designed not to disintegrate, in case they ever needed to exhume her — was lowered into an unmarked grave.

In the years since, modern science has offered a few more clues. Isotope and DNA tests conducted on her remains suggest she grew up in Germany before moving near the French-Belgian border later in life. A carbon-14 test on her teeth also suggested she was closer to forty-five years old, not the twenty-five to thirty she consistently claimed on her hotel cards. After the *Death in Ice Valley* podcast brought new attention to the case, another witness came forward, claiming he saw a woman matching her description hiking near Isdalen just a few days before her body was found, trailed by two very serious-looking men in dark coats. But despite these advances, her true identity and what happened to her in the Valley of Death remain unknown. Her DNA is stored in international databases, holding out the slim hope that a relative might one day come forward and finally give a name to the ghost of the Ice Valley.

20

THE MAN WHO CUT OFF HER ARMS

The road stretched endlessly through the California desert — silent, sun-bleached, and empty. A van slowed to a stop beside a young hitchhiker standing alone on the shoulder. She was fifteen, tired, and just wanted to get home. The man behind the wheel smiled, the kind of harmless, grandfatherly smile that made him seem safe. She climbed in. It was a decision that would change her life forever.

Lawrence Singleton was born in Tampa, Florida, on July 28, 1927. Details about his early life are scarce, but it's known he grew up with numerous siblings. After leaving school, he served in the military during the Korean War, experiencing combat in what was described as a gruesome war zone. Following his military service, he spent most of his working life as a merchant marine, operating machinery below deck on cargo ships and traveling the world.

Singleton married twice, though specifics about these relationships are limited. What is known is that he struggled with alcoholism and exhibited violent tendencies, particularly when drunk. He suffered from depression and had difficulty controlling his anger. Both marriages ended relatively quickly. By his fifties, Singleton had retired from the Merchant Marine service and settled alone in Sparks, Nevada.

He had a daughter from his first marriage, but their relationship was deeply strained. His daughter reportedly disliked him intensely, an animosity fueled by his violent behavior. On one occasion, while drunk, Singleton slapped her hard. Following this incident, his daughter filed a complaint, successfully requested to be removed from his custody, and became estranged from him. This decision, in hindsight, likely saved her from further harm. Beyond these fragments, Lawrence Singleton's life before 1978 remains largely undocumented, offering few clues to the monstrous actions he would later commit.

In the summer of 1978, Mary Vincent's life in Las Vegas was unraveling. Fifteen years old and with six siblings, she had been a bright, talented dancer with aspirations of a professional career. However, her parents were undergoing a difficult divorce, and the turmoil at home led Mary to run away. She began living on the streets, sometimes sleeping in unlocked cars, adrift and vulnerable. For a time, she found companionship with a twenty-six-year-old man named Diego Montoya, but this association ended abruptly when Montoya was arrested for raping another fifteen-year-old girl. Alone again and desperate to escape street life, Mary decided to hitchhike to Los Angeles to stay with her grandfather.

Hitchhiking was common in the 1970s, often perceived as a relatively safe mode of travel. Mary's journey began uneventfully. She caught rides with several different people, making good progress. By September 29, 1978, she had reached Berkeley, California, a college town known for its transient population and frequent hitchhikers. She found herself at a spot colloquially known as "Hitchhiker's Corner," waiting with other young people also heading south.

It was there that Lawrence Singleton, now fifty-one years old, pulled up in his van. To Mary, he looked harmless, like a grandfatherly figure with a friendly smile. He offered her a ride, saying he was also heading south. As Mary climbed in, the other hitchhikers attempted to join her, but Singleton stopped them. He insisted he only had room for one, specifically Mary. This immediately raised red flags for the others at the corner; they warned Mary not to go, sensing something was wrong. But Mary, young, naive, and desperate to reach her destination, ignored their warnings. The fact that Singleton mentioned having a daughter close to her age further reassured her. She climbed into the van, believing the worst that could happen was minimal. It was a decision that would irrevocably alter her life.

Initially, the drive seemed normal. Singleton made small talk, reinforcing the harmless persona. At one point, Mary sneezed after lighting a cigarette. Singleton reached over and stroked her neck. Startled and creeped out, Mary pulled away. Singleton immediately withdrew his hand, and Mary tried to rationalize the odd gesture, telling herself he was perhaps just overly familiar or eccentric. Wanting to avoid confrontation while alone with him, she tried to put the incident out of her mind and eventually fell asleep.

When she awoke sometime later, she instantly knew something was wrong. They were no longer heading south toward Los Angeles; the van was traveling east, toward Nevada. Panic set in as she recalled the earlier warning signs: his insistence on taking only her, the creepy neck stroke, and now the wrong direction. Reaching under her seat, she found a long metal measuring stick. Brandishing it, she demanded Singleton turn around. Surprisingly, he didn't become aggressive. Instead, he acted confused, apologizing profusely, blaming his age and poor sense of direction. He immediately turned the van around and began heading south again. Mary, relieved, relaxed once more, believing she had asserted control.

They drove for some time, eventually reaching a long, deserted stretch of highway. It was now nighttime, and there was barely any other traffic. Suddenly, Singleton slammed on the brakes, announcing he needed to relieve himself. He got out of the van, and Mary exited as well to stretch her legs. Standing on the dark, empty road, a profound sense of unease washed over her. She felt exposed, vulnerable. The thought struck her: *What if he attacks me?* She assessed the situation — he was older, seemingly less fit than her. She believed she could outrun him. Looking down, she noticed her trainers' laces were untied. If she needed to run, she'd need them tied. As she bent down to secure her shoelaces, Lawrence Singleton crept up behind her and brought a sledgehammer down on her head with full force.

Mary lost consciousness instantly. When she came to herself moments later, Singleton was standing over her. He grabbed her hair and forced her to perform oral sex. He then dragged her to the back of the van, tied her up, and proceeded to rape her repeatedly throughout the night. Mary remained conscious through the entire ordeal, screaming, pleading with him to stop, promising she wouldn't tell anyone if he just let her go. He ignored her cries, forcing her to drink an alcoholic substance between assaults, likely to keep her subdued. By sunrise, she was battered, bruised, and bleeding, convinced she was going to die and, in her agony, wishing for it.

As dawn broke, Singleton dragged Mary out of the van and threw her onto the dusty ground beside the deserted road. She continued to plead for her life. "You want to be set free?" Singleton reportedly sneered. "I'll set you free." He went to the back of his van and retrieved a small axe from his toolbox. He returned to Mary, grabbed her left arm, and swung the axe down, severing her forearm just below the elbow in a single, clean blow.

Mary, in shock, felt herself falling backward even as she instinctively tried to hold onto Singleton. Looking down, she saw her left arm was gone. But Singleton wasn't finished. He grabbed her right arm. It took three swings this time, but the result was the same. He chopped off her right forearm. Mary remained conscious, witnessing the horrific act, feeling the searing pain. As she lay on the ground, she looked up and saw her own severed right hand still clamped onto Singleton's arm — her muscles had locked in a death grip at the moment of impact. She watched him frantically shake his arm, trying to dislodge the gruesome appendage.

Once free of her severed hand, Singleton dragged Mary's mutilated body to a nearby ravine and threw her over the edge, a drop of some thirty feet (about nine meters). Still not satisfied, he carefully climbed down the embankment to where she lay. To ensure she wouldn't be found, he shoved her broken body into a concrete drainage pipe, assuming she would bleed out and her remains would remain hidden. Then, he climbed back up, got in his van, and drove away, leaving the fifteen-year-old girl for dead.

Against all odds, Mary Vincent did not die. Lying in the cold concrete pipe, bleeding profusely, weak, and freezing as night fell again, she fought the overwhelming urge to succumb to sleep. A voice in her head, she later recalled, urged her to stay awake, telling her she had to survive to stop this man from hurting anyone else. Fueled by this thought, she somehow found the strength to push herself out of the pipe.

Once free, her survival instincts took over. Realizing she would bleed to death if she didn't stop the flow from her severed arms, she did something remarkable. She plunged the stumps of her arms into the surrounding mud. The mixture of blood and earth created a crude paste, which she packed into the wounds, effectively creating clots that slowed, then stopped the bleeding. It also, she later said, kept her muscles from protruding from the raw ends of her arms.

Her next challenge was the cliff. Without hands or forearms, weak from blood loss and trauma, she began the arduous climb. Using the bones protruding from her arms and her feet, she dragged herself up the steep embankment. It took her an entire day, an agonizing, inch-by-inch struggle against gravity and exhaustion, but she made it to the top.

Back on the deserted road, she could hear the faint sound of traffic in the distance. She began walking toward the sound, another journey that took miles and hours in her ravaged state. Finally, she reached the side of a slightly busier road, though still remote. She stood there, battered, covered in dried blood and mud, armless, hoping for rescue.

The first car that approached, a red convertible, slowed down, the occupants clearly seeing her horrific condition, but then sped away. Mary later expressed understanding, acknowledging she must have looked like something from a nightmare. But shortly after, another convertible appeared. This couple, on their honeymoon and lost, did stop. They bundled Mary into their car, tried to tend to her wounds, and raced to find a phone. Paramedics arrived, and Mary was airlifted to a hospital equipped to handle her catastrophic injuries. Doctors determined she had lost nearly half the blood in her body, and what remained had reached toxic levels. Incredibly, she survived.

Mary's physical recovery was long and grueling. Surgeons grafted muscle from her legs to reconstruct parts of her arms. She was fitted with prosthetic arms ending in hooks. During the investigation, in a bizarre postscript, police found one of Mary's severed arms washed up near the Golden Gate Bridge in San Francisco, over a hundred miles from the attack site, far too late for reattachment.

Initially, Mary was too traumatized to speak coherently about the attack. Police employed forensic hypnosis to help her recall the details. Gradually, she provided an accurate description of Lawrence Singleton. The resulting composite sketch was so precise that Singleton's own neighbor recognized him and called the police. On October 9, 1978, just two weeks after the attack, Lawrence Singleton was arrested. Mary identified him in a lineup.

Confronted by police, Singleton denied everything. He concocted a story about picking up Mary along with two other male hitchhikers named "Pedro" and "Larry." He claimed they all went to a bar, smoked marijuana, and then paid Mary $10 each for sex, calling her a "cheap prostitute." He denied raping her or cutting off her arms, blaming the fictitious Pedro and Larry. Police saw through the lies immediately.

A search of Singleton's home revealed remnants of Mary's burnt clothing and a pack of her cigarettes. He had ripped out the carpet in his van and meticulously cleaned it, attempting to remove all traces of blood. Investigators also learned he had attempted suicide shortly after the attack, which they interpreted as a sign of guilt.

The trial took place in March 1979. Mary Vincent faced her attacker in court, taking the stand just feet away from him. As she walked past Singleton after delivering her harrowing testimony, he leaned toward her and whispered a chilling threat: "If it's the last thing I do, I will finish the job."

The jury found Lawrence Singleton guilty on all charges: kidnapping, mutilation, attempted murder, forcible rape, sodomy, and forced oral copulation. Despite the severity and number of convictions, the sentence was shockingly lenient. Due to sentencing laws in California at the time, the maximum penalty he could receive was just fourteen years. He was sent to San Quentin State Prison.

Mary tried to rebuild her life, but the trauma, coupled with the knowledge that her attacker would eventually be released, cast a long shadow. Sadly, her family struggled to cope with her injuries and the aftermath of the attack, and she eventually became estranged from them. She got engaged and had two children, but the approach of Singleton's potential release date caused her immense stress. Then, on her wedding day, she received devastating news: Lawrence Singleton was being released after serving only eight years. He had earned early release for "good behavior" and through a work incentive program designed to alleviate prison overcrowding. A psychological evaluation conducted just before his release deemed him "out of touch with his hostility and anger" and an "elevated threat," yet he was freed anyway.

Singleton's release sparked public outrage. No community in California wanted him. Protests erupted wherever parole officials tried to place him. Residents picketed his temporary residences, firebombed his brother's house where he briefly stayed, and demanded he leave. Eventually, officials resorted to housing him in a trailer on the grounds of San Quentin for the duration of his one-year parole. The public outcry led to the passage of the "Singleton Bill" in California, increasing penalties for crimes involving torture and limiting early release for such offenders, though it couldn't be applied retroactively to Singleton himself.

After his parole ended, Singleton moved back to his hometown of Tampa, Florida. He faced similar rejection there but eventually found a place to live, largely keeping his past hidden. Mary, meanwhile, struggled. Her marriage ended, she fell into debt, her health suffered, and she could no longer afford upkeep on her prosthetics. In a display of staggering audacity, Singleton sued Mary from Florida, absurdly claiming *he* was the victim of kidnapping by her and the fictional Pedro and Larry. The suit went nowhere. Mary countersued and won a $2.56 million judgment, but Singleton only had $200 to his name.

Over the next decade, Singleton lived a mostly quiet, lonely life in Florida, punctuated by minor crimes, including a brief return to prison for stealing a $3 hat. Neighbors described him as a raging alcoholic, rumored to drink two gallons of vodka a day. His health declined, and he reportedly battled cancer. In February 1997, a neighbor found him attempting suicide and intervened, saving his life — an act the neighbor would later bitterly regret.

Just days after the suicide attempt, on February 19, 1997, Lawrence Singleton, now sixty-nine, picked up Roxanne Hayes, a thirty-one-year-old mother of three working as a sex worker to fund a drug addiction. Roxanne had endured a difficult life, surviving childhood sexual and physical abuse and the death of her mother. Despite her struggles, she was known as a witty, caring person devoted to her children.

Singleton took Roxanne back to his home. Around 6:00 p.m., the neighbor who had recently saved Singleton's life came by to discuss some work. Peering through the window after getting no answer at the door, he witnessed a horrifying scene: Singleton, naked and covered in blood, standing over Roxanne, beating and strangling her. Roxanne was still alive and screaming for help. The neighbor banged on the window, momentarily distracting Singleton, who stared blankly at him before turning back to continue the assault. The neighbor immediately called 911.

When a deputy arrived, Singleton answered the door, still naked and blood-soaked. He claimed he had cut his finger while chopping vegetables. The deputy stepped inside and found Roxanne Hayes's lifeless body on the living room floor. She had been beaten, strangled, and stabbed multiple times.

Lawrence Singleton was arrested and charged with first-degree murder. This time, he didn't deny the killing but tried to justify it, claiming Roxanne had tried to steal from him. Many theorized, however, that the murder was a surrogate act — unable to fulfill his threat against Mary Vincent, he unleashed his rage on a woman who bore a striking resemblance to her. His approach was also different: brazen, in his own home, with no attempt at concealment, suggesting perhaps he no longer cared about getting caught.

At Singleton's trial for the murder of Roxanne Hayes, Mary Vincent emerged from hiding. She took the stand once more, testifying about her own horrific experience at his hands. Coupled with the neighbor's eyewitness account and the overwhelming physical evidence, the testimony ensured Singleton's conviction. This time, his sentence was death.

Lawrence Singleton died of cancer on Florida's death row in 2001 before his execution could be carried out. Mary Vincent, upon hearing the news, found closure not in his death itself, but in the relief she saw on her children's faces. Singleton could no longer harm them. She remarried and dedicated herself to advocacy, setting up a foundation for victims of traumatic crime and sharing her story publicly to inspire others. She also discovered a talent for painting, selling her artwork.

While Mary found a path to healing and purpose, Roxanne Hayes's life was tragically cut short, leaving behind three children. Investigators suspected Singleton likely had other victims over the years, perhaps during his decades traveling as a merchant marine, but no definitive links were ever established. His documented acts against Mary Vincent and Roxanne Hayes remain a chilling testament to his capacity for extreme, inexplicable violence.

21

THE ANGELS OF INSURANCE

In a quiet corner of Kansas, just north of Wichita, lay a ten-acre (about 40,500 square meters) farm known as Angel's Landing. To outsiders, it was a place of surprising wealth and idyllic freedom. The commune hosted lavish parties, with guests swimming in the large pool or riding ATVs on a private track. A fleet of expensive cars — Dodge Vipers, Corvettes, and multiple SUVs with personalized "Angel" license plates — shuttled members around town. The children living there seemed to have everything, including multiple horses.

At the center of this makeshift family was Lou Castro, a man who was, by his own account, a centuries-old angel. He was a jack-of-all-trades in the supernatural realm: he claimed to be possessed by three separate angels, he could predict the future, and he even held the power to bring the dead back to life. But this lavish lifestyle had a dark price, one paid by Lou's own followers. Every few years, like clockwork, a member of the commune would die in a bizarre and tragic accident. As the body count grew, this supposed paradise began to look less like a sanctuary and more like a hunting ground.

The path to Angel's Landing began for one family in 2001, in a suburb of Kansas City, Missouri. The Hudson family was living a typical, happy life.

Jennifer Hudson was a real estate agent, often selling the houses her husband built. They had two daughters: Sarah, a seventeen-year-old self-proclaimed daddy's girl with a rebellious streak, and Emily, a ten-year-old top student. The girls were close despite their age gap, and the family ate dinner together every night. Their life was stable and unremarkable until the summer of 2001, when Jennifer took on a new client named Lou Castro.

Lou and his companions, a married couple named Trish and Brian Hughes, and another woman known only as KL, were looking for a large property to accommodate their group. Lou described them as a makeshift family of free spirits, living in harmony. Jennifer, herself a very spiritual person with a fascination for angels, was immediately captivated. Lou was charming, soft-spoken, and exuded a calm, dignified air. He told her he was independently wealthy from the stock market and owning cattle, which explained his expensive cars and mansion.

As their friendship progressed, Lou revealed his truth: he was a centuries-old angel and seer. He claimed he could see the future, know the date of a person's death, change the weather, and was a relative of Geronimo. His followers backed up every claim. Trish Hughes, his second in command, swore to Jennifer that she had personally witnessed Lou bring an animal, and even himself, back from the dead. Trish told Jennifer, "People say you can't pick your family, but that's exactly what we've done," and invited her to join.

The allure of this new life quickly fractured the old one. Jennifer's once-solid marriage began to crumble, and soon, she and her husband divorced. Lou and his group moved to a ten-acre (about 40,500 square meters) property in Kansas, and Jennifer, telling her daughters she couldn't stand to be far from him, announced they were moving. She promised the girls that Lou, being an angel, would protect them. In the fall of 2001, Jennifer packed up her two daughters and drove them to Angel's Landing to start a new life. Their father, devastated, eventually moved to Kansas just to be closer to his children.

The commune was a small group. At the top was Lou Castro, who claimed to be possessed by three angels: Arthur, the bad angel; Daniel, the nice one; and Amber, the angel of death. Trish Hughes was second in command, a happy, laughing woman who had known Lou for years. Her husband, Brian, was a diesel mechanic, deeply devoted to his wife and their daughter. Then there was KL, a woman who had met Lou in 1996 when she was just fifteen and he was forty-six, a relationship that had begun as illegal abuse but which she, at the time, believed was consensual.

At first, Sarah and Emily were miserable. Sarah, seventeen, despised Lou for breaking up her family. Emily, at ten, was easier to win over. Lou showered them with gifts, a tactic known as love bombing. Emily was given three horses; anything the girls wanted, Lou provided. As time went on, Sarah's guard came down. She saw how happy her mother was and how much everyone else loved and trusted Lou, and she too grew to care for him. Jennifer found a real estate job in the area, and in her absence, Trish stepped in as a second mother to the girls, helping them all settle into one big, seemingly happy family.

But the idyllic facade hid a nightmarish reality. Almost immediately, Lou began sexually abusing ten-year-old Emily. He manipulated her with a terrifying story: as an ancient angel, he could only survive by being sexual with a young girl. He told her she was special and gave him the power he needed to stay alive. He recited Bible scriptures to justify his actions, convincing the child that if she refused, this man she had grown to love would die, and it would be her fault. Just weeks after arriving, Emily began sharing Lou's bed every night, a routine that continued for years.

She was not his only victim. He also manipulated and abused seventeen-year-old Sarah. He told her she was "broken" and that if she ever wanted a family of her own, she had to have sex with him so he could "fix" her. He enforced her silence by threatening that if she ever told anyone, something terrible would happen to her father, the man she adored. He was also abusing KL, and at times would force all three girls to engage in activities with each other. He referred to this abuse as "feeding," claiming it was time for him to feed. He pitted the sisters against each other, straining their relationship, and would fly into violent rages, blaming the "bad angel" Arthur for his actions.

The other adults in the commune claimed to know nothing. Emily later said that because she and Lou were so close, no one found it strange when they disappeared together. But the fact that Jennifer allowed her ten-year-old daughter to sleep in a grown man's bed every night suggests the depth of Lou's control, or her own complicity. It's likely Lou targeted Jennifer from the beginning, seducing her into the group to gain unlimited access to her daughters.

This pattern of abuse and control was funded by a far more lethal operation. Before the Hudsons ever arrived, Lou's inner circle had already experienced its first "tragedy." In February 2001, a woman named Mona Griffith, a single mother of two named Cody and Lindsay, died in a plane crash. Mona had become close friends with Trish and Lou in the mid-90s in Corpus Christi, Texas, and moved with them to South Dakota. She, her daughter Lindsay, and her new boyfriend, a fifty-year-old real estate agent named Jim Chase, were on a trip to Nebraska in Jim's private plane when it vanished. The wreckage was found six weeks later; there were no survivors.

After the crash, Lou came into a large sum of money. At his direction, Mona had taken out a $750,000 life insurance policy on herself, naming her daughter Lindsay as the beneficiary. She had also, at Lou's direction, named Trish Hughes as Lindsay's guardian. With both Mona and Lindsay dead, the money was awarded to Trish and promptly handed over to Lou. This was his true business: he wasn't a stock trader; he was a con artist who funded his lavish lifestyle through insurance payouts. He had every adult in the cult take out large policies on themselves, carefully instructing them who to name as beneficiaries so that his own name was never attached.

By the summer of 2003, just two years after Mona's death, Lou's bank account was running low. Around this time, a narcotics detective named Ron Goodwin had already begun looking into Angel's Landing. The unexplained wealth smelled like a drug case, but Goodwin was baffled to find no record of a "Lou Castro" anywhere. The houses and cars were all registered in the names of other cult members. Goodwin suspected "Lou Castro" was an alias and made it his mission to find out who the man really was.

He didn't know that Lou was already planning his next windfall. One night, Lou approached Trish, her toddler daughter, and eleven-year-old

Emily with a solemn announcement: he had a vision. Amber, the angel of death, had shown him that it was Trish's time to die. Emily was hysterical, but Trish, a deep believer, remained perfectly calm. She assured Emily that it was fine, that Lou would simply bring her back to life after she died, healthier than ever.

A week later, the group went out to lunch. When they returned to Angel's Landing, Lou instructed Trish and Emily to clean the pool. He and Sarah, meanwhile, would go car shopping, securing his alibi. While Sarah was inside getting ready, Lou walked Emily, Trish, and Trish's toddler to the pool. He told Emily the time had come and instructed her to take the baby into a nearby workshop and wait. Emily, crying, hugged Trish goodbye on the diving board. A few minutes after Emily was in the workshop, she heard a splash and a scream. It is believed Lou hit Trish over the head, knocking her into the pool, and then held her underwater until she drowned. The small bruises found on her forehead during the autopsy were not from the fall, but from Lou's fingers pressing into her skin.

A few minutes later, Lou entered the workshop, out of breath and with wet arms, and gave Emily her instructions. She was to wait twenty minutes, then get in the pool with the baby so they would both be wet. She was to call 911 and tell them Trish's daughter had fallen in, and that Trish had slipped, hit her head, and drowned while trying to save her. Emily, terrified, did exactly as she was told, getting into the water where her surrogate mother's body was floating face down. When Lou and Sarah raced back, police were already there. Trish's death was ruled a tragic accident. Lou collected over $1 million in insurance payouts. Three months later, he donated $19,000 to the local police department for a new patrol car, with the sole request that it bear a sticker in memory of Patricia Hughes.

The cycle repeated. Three years later, in late 2006, the money was low again. The next to die was Brian Hughes, Trish's grieving husband. Lou had spent months manipulating the despondent man, telling him that "crossing over" was the ultimate, peaceful goal. While visiting family in South Dakota, Brian, a diesel mechanic known for his obsessive attention to safety, was crushed to death when a jack allegedly gave out and a vehicle fell on him. He hadn't used cinder blocks under the tires, something he normally always did. Lou, back in Kansas, had been heard commenting that he did not expect Brian to return from the trip. It was believed Lou had convinced Brian it was his time, allowing him one last trip to see his family before staging his own death.

Two years later, in 2008, the accounts were low again. This time, Lou's vision was for Jennifer Hudson. When he told Sarah and Emily, they protested, but their mother, still a true believer, calmly told them it was okay and not to worry. Not long after, Jennifer Hudson died on impact when she slammed her car at high speed into a gravel truck. Witnesses all said the same thing: it looked as though she had deliberately swerved into oncoming traffic. The girls knew their mother was never coming back; they had waited for years for Trish and Brian to be resurrected, and they never were.

In 2009, Lou moved the remnants of his cult to a large colonial house in Columbia, Tennessee. Sarah, now twenty-four, refused to go, choosing to stay in Kansas near her father. Lou left with Emily, then seventeen, and his other followers. Finally free from Lou's constant control, Sarah began to breathe. She started dating a man named Daniel McGrath, and as she slowly revealed the story of her life, he became justifiably alarmed. Without telling Sarah, Daniel McGrath wrote a secret email to the FBI, detailing the years of abuse, the mysterious deaths, the insurance payouts, and Lou's new location in Tennessee.

This was the break investigators had been waiting for. The FBI began surveillance on the Tennessee home and saw a vehicle registered to a "Joe Venegas." They monitored Lou's bank accounts, watching money transfer from Kansas to Tennessee. At the Tennessee bank, security footage captured Lou and Emily opening an account under the false name Joe Venegas. It was identity fraud, and it was enough. In April 2010, detectives arrested Lou at his home. He was arrogant, but his fingerprints, when run, came up empty. He was booked as a John Doe, pleaded guilty to identity fraud, and was sentenced to two years in prison, likely believing this would end the investigation.

It only gave detectives the time they needed. They focused on Trish Hughes, who had known Lou the longest. They called her family in Beeville, Texas, and her sister told them about a man Trish had dated in the 90s named Daniel Perez, who had reportedly died. On a hunch, detectives requested records for Daniel Perez. As Detective Goodwin stood by the fax machine, a mugshot printed out. Staring back at him was Lou Castro.

They finally had his real identity. Daniel Perez, born in 1959, was a former army plane mechanic — a detail that made the 2001 plane crash infinitely more suspicious. They also learned *why* he had "died." In the mid-90s, Perez had pleaded no contest to the sexual assault of two young girls, but the charges were dropped when he was reported dead after a beating. He had faked his death, and Trish, who was just a teenager when she met him, was his first follower. Together, they became Lou and Trish and began collecting new members and new insurance policies.

With Lou in prison, his psychological hold began to break. Sarah gave investigators a full account, including a story of how Lou had threatened to kill her father unless she secretly videotaped an eight-year-old girl undressing. Emily, however, remained loyal. Her loyalty finally shattered when she wrote Lou a letter in prison, telling him she was happy and doing well. Lou wrote back, furiously berating her for daring to find happiness without him. That cruelty was the final snap. Emily started talking, telling detectives the true, step-by-step story of how Lou Castro murdered Trish Hughes.

When Daniel Perez was released from prison for identity fraud, he was immediately rearrested and charged with twenty-eight new felonies, including the exploitation of a child, assault, and the first-degree murder of Trish Hughes. His trial began in early 2015. Sarah, Emily, and four other women, all unconnected to each other, took the stand and told nearly identical stories of abuse at his hands. Lou took the stand in his own defense, spinning a web of bizarre lies. He claimed he hadn't faked his death but had been beaten, suffered amnesia, and it was Trish who convinced him his name was Lou. He claimed he never abused anyone but had consensual sex with them as adults. He said Amber, Arthur, and Daniel weren't angels, just names he liked to be called during intimacy.

The jury did not believe him. He was found guilty on all charges and sentenced to eighty years in prison without the possibility of parole. He is currently serving his time at the Lansing Correctional Facility in Kansas. In the wake of the trial, both Sarah and Emily Hudson have gotten married and are focused on healing from the youth that was stolen from them.

22

CHILDREN OF THUNDER

At 5:00 a.m. on August 2nd, 2000, the sound of gunfire echoed through the small town of Woodacre, California. Police were dispatched to a small studio apartment, a unit tucked away behind the garage of a main house, difficult to find unless one already knew it was there. Inside, officers found a grisly scene. Ginny Villarin, forty-five, was dead on the bed. Her boyfriend, fifty-four-year-old Jim Gamble, was on the floor beside her. Both were naked and had been shot multiple times. The room was soaked in blood, and 6.9-mm shell casings littered the floor. Yet, two separate stashes of money were found untouched in the apartment. This was not a robbery; it was an execution.

The victims had been house-sitting. The apartment belonged to Ginny's twenty-three-year-old daughter, Selena Bishop. Ginny and Jim had gone there to sleep after Ginny finished her late shift at a local bar, the Paper Mill Creek Saloon. Ginny Villarin was a beloved figure, the long-ago girlfriend of famed musician Elvin Bishop, who had famously written the song "Fooled Around and Fell in Love" about her. Though they had split in the early 80s, Ginny remained the vibrant center of her family. Jim Gamble was a retired and charismatic man from Napa Valley, a longtime friend who had driven to Pennsylvania in 1999 to help Ginny move back to California. Their old friendship had recently turned into a romance.

The investigation immediately focused on the apartment's absent tenant, Selena Bishop. She was supposedly on a camping trip in Yosemite with a mysterious new boyfriend known only as "Jordan," a man she had kept hidden from her friends and family. Selena's journal entries revealed her deep unease with this new man: "There is so much of your life hidden from me," she wrote. "Your name, your past, your wife... I realize I don't know you from a can of paint... I won't want to be with you when your big plan goes down. I don't want to be rich."

When Selena failed to show up for her 10:30 a.m. shift at the Two Bird Cafe on Friday, August 5th, she was officially declared a missing person. The case broke open when her coworkers found a pager she had forgotten at the cafe. Detectives scrolling through the numbers found one with a Concord, California area code, registered to a man named Justin Helser. Investigators learned that Justin lived with his older brother, Taylor Helser, and that Justin had recently purchased a 9-mm handgun — the same caliber used to murder Ginny and Jim. When police showed a bartender at a place Selena frequented a photo of Taylor Helser, he immediately identified him. "Jordan," he said.

Glenn Taylor Helser and his younger brother Justin were raised in a devout Mormon household, but the family dynamic was deeply unhealthy. Their mother, Karma, who was believed to have undiagnosed mental health issues, became convinced that her eldest son, Taylor, was a prophet. She encouraged the entire family to defer to him, and Justin, who was more introverted, grew up idolizing and obeying his older brother. Taylor was charismatic and a rising star in the church, setting conversion records on his mission trip to Brazil in 1989. But the trip also radicalized him; he became obsessed with the "moral decay" of the world, the coming apocalypse, and his own belief that he had a direct line to God.

When Taylor returned home in 1991, his mother introduced him to a controversial self-help program called Harmony Impact Training. The program's mantra was that there was "no right and no wrong," only "results." It used cult-like tactics, including sleep deprivation, public humiliation, and intense psychological games, to break members down before building them back up. Taylor, who had married his high school girlfriend and become a stockbroker, embraced this new philosophy. He grew bored with his family, telling a psychiatrist he resented his wife for not being as sexually submissive as the women he saw in pornography and confessing his fantasy of gathering a group of Brazilian women to be his sex slaves.

In 1996, Taylor left his wife and children and moved in with Justin, immediately forcing his brother to attend the Harmony training. After Taylor was excommunicated from the Mormon church for drug use and his extreme beliefs, his delusions fully crystallized. He and Justin would save the world by taking over the Mormon church, which they would accomplish by training an army of Brazilian orphan assassins to kill the church leaders. To fund this plan, Taylor estimated he would need $20 million.

Taylor and Justin formed a small cult with a new recruit, Dawn Godman, a vulnerable woman with a history of meth addiction and homelessness whom Taylor had met at a church function. He charmed her, took her to the parking lot of a Mormon temple, and told her he was a prophet; she believed him. Taylor named the trio the "Children of Thunder," with himself in the role of Jesus. He armed them with his "Twelve Principles of Magic," including the tenets: "I am already perfect and therefore can do nothing wrong" and "I am always right."

Their plan for raising money was extortion. First, they needed a clean bank account. Taylor, using the alias "Jordan," met twenty-two-year-old Selena Bishop at a rave. He love-bombed her and fed her a story about needing to hide a $100,000 inheritance from his "ex-wife." Believing him, Selena opened a new bank account in her name on June 30, 2000.

The cult's first targets were eighty-five-year-old Ivan and seventy-eight-year-old Annette Steinman, a wealthy, elderly couple who had been Taylor's clients during his stockbroker days. On July 30, 2000, the Children of Thunder declared war on Satan in a group prayer, and then Taylor and Justin went to the Steinmans' home. The couple let them in, and Justin pulled the 9-mm handgun. The brothers forced the terrified couple into their own minivan and drove them to the cult's house in Concord.

There, the trio forced the Steinmans to ingest Rohypnol and handcuffed them. They were forced to write checks — Ivan for $33,000 and Annette for $67,000 — made out to Selena Bishop. When Annette began to nod off from the drugs, Taylor forced her to smoke meth, blowing the smoke into her face to keep her conscious enough to sign the check. Believing the drugs would kill the couple, the cult members waited, but the elderly couple proved resilient. Impatient, Taylor ordered the group to strip to their underwear to avoid bloodstains. He and Justin began bashing the couple's heads against the bathroom floor, but they both fought back. Taylor then slit Annette's throat with a hunting knife; when she still struggled, he pulled her head back and drowned her in her own blood. Ivan continued to fight as Dawn sat on his chest until he suffered a fatal heart attack. The cult members then dismembered the bodies and packed them into duffel bags.

The plan unraveled the next day, July 31st. Dawn went to the bank in an outlandish disguise — a bright green sweatsuit, pigtails, a cowboy hat, and a wheelchair — to deposit the checks. She told the bank manager, Vicki Sexton, a convoluted story about Selena needing emergency heart surgery. Sexton, highly suspicious, put a hold on the checks and tried to call the Steinmans but got no answer. Dawn left empty-handed. The cult realized they had made a critical error: they had killed the Steinmans before the checks had cleared.

They now had to eliminate the only remaining loose end: Selena Bishop. On August 2nd, Selena came to Taylor's house, believing she was about to leave for her camping trip. Taylor told her to lie down for a back rub. As she lay on the floor, Justin crept into the room and repeatedly struck her in the head with a hammer. As Dawn began to clean the blood, she noticed Selena's legs were still moving. Taylor dragged the dying woman to the bathroom, put her in the tub, slit her throat, and held her head underwater until she was dead.

But Taylor wasn't finished. He decided Selena's mother, Ginny, also had to die, as she had briefly seen him once at Selena's apartment. That same night, he and Dawn drove to Woodacre. Taylor, dressed in a long black coat and carrying two guns, used his key to enter Selena's apartment. He was startled to find Jim Gamble in bed with Ginny, and he immediately opened fire, killing them both. He and Dawn then returned to Concord, where Taylor cut the tattoo from Selena's shoulder and fed it to his Rottweiler to hinder identification. The remains of Selena and the Steinmans were packed into nine duffel bags and dumped into the Sacramento River Delta.

On August 7th, after bank manager Vicki Sexton linked the Steinman checks to the missing Selena, and Selena's pager led police to the Helser brothers, authorities raided the Concord home. They arrested Justin and Dawn, and captured Taylor after he fled, broke into a neighbor's home, and threatened a woman with a knife. That same day, a jet skier on the Sacramento River Delta discovered the first of the nine duffel bags containing the dismembered victims.

Once in custody, Dawn Godman was worked with by a cult deprogrammer. Realizing she had been brainwashed, she testified against the brothers and was sentenced to thirty-eight years in prison. Taylor Helser, who remained defiant, described the murders as "collateral damage" and the work of a soldier in a holy war. He was given five death sentences and remains on death row. Justin Helser was given three death sentences. In 2013, after several previous attempts, including stabbing himself in the eyes with pencils, Justin Helser was found hanging in his cell, dead by suicide.

23

THE GIRL IN DARK CANYON

In August 2010, nearly a year after twenty-four-year-old Mitrice Richardson vanished, park rangers were hiking through Dark Canyon, an incredibly steep and remote area in the Malibu hills. The terrain was so difficult that it was not recommended for hikers. There, they discovered a human skull with dark, curly hair still attached. Nearby were women's clothes. The remains were soon confirmed to be those of Mitrice. The discovery, however, raised far more questions than it answered. Her body was found in a state that baffled investigators: her shirts, underwear, socks, and shoes were missing, yet her remains, which had lain exposed for almost a year in an area full of coyotes and scavengers, were almost completely undisturbed by animals.

Before she was a set of remains in a canyon, Mitrice Richardson was a bright and ambitious woman. Born in 1985, she was raised by her mother, Latice Sutton, and her great-grandmother, Mildred. Her biological father, Michael Richardson, had been incarcerated for drug dealing when she was four. Seeking a quieter life away from the 1993 LA riots, the family moved to the suburbs of Covina, where Mitrice thrived. She was a high-achieving student who found school almost too easy. She was a cheerleader and loved to dance, known for a happy, contagious energy. She was the first in her family to attend college, graduating with honors from Cal State Fullerton in 2008 with a degree in psychology. She planned to pursue her master's degree while living with her great-grandmother and working as a "go-go" dancer under the name "Hazel" at a local nightclub.

In the summer of 2009, Mitrice's behavior began to change. Friends and family noticed she seemed stressed and withdrawn, possibly due to a complicated relationship with a woman named Vanessa. She stopped calling friends and instead sent bizarre, disjointed text messages. Her social media was filled with random, philosophical statements posted at all hours. In one text to her mother, she claimed she wanted to be "Miss Mother Nature" and needed to talk to Michelle Obama about creating a position for her in the White House. On September 16, 2009, she went to her shipping company job, seemed fine, but left at lunch and never returned. That evening, she skipped her regular Wednesday dinner with her great-grandmother, saying the ocean was "calling her name" and she was driving to Malibu.

Mitrice arrived in Malibu and pulled into the parking lot of Geoffrey's, an expensive, valet-only restaurant. Her behavior was immediately erratic. She climbed into a valet's personal car, telling the confused employee it was "subliminal" and that she was there to "avenge the death of Michael Jackson." She walked into the restaurant wearing a Bob Marley T-shirt and a Rastafarian hat. After ordering a $65 Kobe steak and a cocktail, she joined a table of seven strangers, telling them she was from another planet. When her meal was finished, she attempted to walk out with the group, leaving her $90 bill unpaid. Stopped by the manager, she emptied her pockets and said, "I'm busted. What are we gonna do?" The restaurant staff, believing she was on drugs or having a mental crisis, called the police. Mitrice's great-grandmother, Mildred, called and offered to pay the bill over the phone, but the restaurant refused to accept it without her being physically present.

When deputies from the LA Sheriff's station arrived, Mitrice passed a sobriety test. They searched her car and found her driver's license and a small, non-arrestable amount of marijuana. Her wallet, phone, and debit card were all in the messy vehicle. The restaurant owner, however, insisted on pressing charges for defrauding an innkeeper. Mitrice was handcuffed and taken to the station. Her mother, Latice, called the station and was explicitly told that Mitrice would be held overnight; the officer assured her they would have Mitrice call in the morning. Relieved, Latice went to sleep, believing her daughter was, at the very least, safe. Despite Mitrice's bizarre behavior, deputies made no notes about her mental state, a decision that would later be debated as a way to avoid paperwork. At 12:15 a.m. on September 17, Mitrice was released. She was alone, in the dark, with no car, no money, and no phone. Her impounded car was fifteen miles (about twenty-four kilometers) away. The department later claimed she had refused offers to stay in the lobby.

At 5:20 a.m., Latice called the station, only to be told her daughter had been released hours earlier. Panicked, she tried to file a missing persons report but was told to wait twenty-four hours. An hour later, at 6:30 a.m., a retired reporter named Bill Smith, living in the remote Monte Nido canyon area six miles (about ten kilometers) from the station, called 911. He reported a slim Black woman with an afro in his backyard, who said she was "just resting" before disappearing. A deputy was dispatched but found no one. The first official search didn't happen for another forty-eight hours, according to the family. A tracking dog picked up Mitrice's scent at Smith's home but quickly lost it.

The investigation was immediately fraught with tension. The Sheriff's department denied any negligence, drawing public fury when it was pointed out that actor Mel Gibson had been arrested at the same station for a driving under influence (DUI) charge and was given a courtesy ride back to his car. For months, the department insisted that there was no surveillance footage of Mitrice in her cell, claiming the cameras didn't record. Only after her family's attorney applied heavy pressure did the footage "magically" appear, showing Mitrice acting agitated in her cell, and, crucially, a deputy exiting the station at the exact moment she was released, contradicting the official report.

The discovery of her remains in August 2010 only deepened the mystery. The scene was so remote that the coroner could not access it, and the body had to be airlifted. The only scene photographs were taken on a park ranger's cell phone. The official cause of death was ruled "undetermined," with no signs of trauma. This conclusion was fiercely disputed. Mitrice's family hired a forensic anthropologist who pointed out glaring inconsistencies. The Sheriff's department claimed the body was "untouched," yet her skull was detached and five of her neck bones were missing. Her left arm was flexed in a position that defied gravity, suggesting homicide, not an accidental death. Her teeth had a pinkish hue, a potential sign of strangulation, but the missing neck bones made confirmation impossible. An earring she was not reported to be wearing was found tangled in her hair, but it was never examined.

Mitrice's parents, Latice Sutton and Michael Richardson, both filed separate lawsuits against the LA Sheriff's Department for negligence and were awarded settlements. The department, however, never admitted any wrongdoing. A subsequent investigation by the California Attorney General's office found insufficient evidence to charge any deputies with a crime, in part because the statute of limitations had already expired. The case remains unsolved, suspended between theories of a tragic accident fueled by a mental health crisis, or a homicide cover-up, all of which began the moment deputies released a vulnerable woman into the pitch-black, unfamiliar canyon roads with no way to get home.

24

THE MISSING SECRETARY

Mary Shotwell Little was twenty-five years old and settling into a new life. A secretary at the Citizens & Southern National Bank in Atlanta, Georgia, she had been married for just six weeks to Roy Little, a bank auditor. On the morning of October 14, 1965, her husband was out of town, having traveled sixty miles (about ninety-six kilometers) south of the city for a work training course, leaving Mary at their home alone. Her day proceeded as expected: she completed her shift at the bank, went grocery shopping, and then, with her evening free, made plans to meet a friend.

She drove her 1965 metallic pearl gray Comet to the Lenox Square Shopping Center, one of Atlanta's more affluent destinations, known for its expensive shops and "posh" restaurants. It was not the kind of place where residents feared for their safety. Mary met a co-worker at the Piccadilly Cafeteria, and they shared a pleasant dinner. The co-worker later recalled that Mary was in high spirits, talking happily about her new married life and seeming to be in a very happy place.

At approximately 8:00 p.m., the women left the restaurant and walked back into the car park. The area was well-lit and still busy with other patrons leaving for the evening. Since they were parked in different areas, the friends parted ways. Mary's last words to her co-worker were a simple "see you," which the friend assumed meant she would see her at work the next day. It was the last time anyone is known to have seen her.

The next morning, October 15, Mary did not show up for work. This was immediately alarming; she was known for being punctual, and her failure to arrive was completely out of character. Her worried boss first tried calling her home, but the line rang unanswered. He then contacted her landlady, who checked the apartment and reported that Mary's morning newspaper was still on the doorstep, a strong indication that she had never made it home the previous night.

After speaking with the co-worker Mary had dined with, the boss called Lenox Square security and asked them to search the car park for Mary's gray Comet. The security guards, who had started their shift at 6:00 a.m., reported that the car was not there. A patrol police officer who had also driven through the lot that morning confirmed their account: the car was gone. Frustrated and increasingly concerned, Mary's boss drove to Lenox Square himself around midday. He began his own search of the car park and, within minutes, found it. Mary's 1965 Comet was parked in the lot in plain sight. The discovery posed an immediate and baffling question: Had the security guards and the police officer somehow missed the car, or had it been taken and returned sometime between 6:00 a.m. and midday?

Police were dispatched to the scene, and Roy Little was finally contacted at his training course and rushed back to Atlanta. The scene inside the car was bizarre and deeply unsettling. The vehicle's exterior was coated in a thin layer of red dust, suggesting it had recently been driven at high speed down a dirt road. Inside, Mary's four bags of groceries from the previous night sat undisturbed. Also present were bottles of Coke and a pack of Kent cigarettes, her preferred brand.

The most disturbing evidence, however, was a small pile of clothing. Mary's slip, panties, and girdle had been neatly folded and placed on the center console between the two front seats. On the floorboard lay her bra and one of her stockings. The stocking appeared to have been cut with a knife. The undergarments, which were confirmed to belong to Mary and to have been recently worn, were speckled with blood. More blood was found smeared on the steering wheel, the driver's side door handle, and the passenger side window.

Forensic analysis determined the blood was almost certainly Mary's, but the quantity was small, not enough to suggest a fatal wound, perhaps as little as would come from a small nosebleed. The way the blood was smeared, combined with the unnaturally tidy stack of underwear, led many officers to believe the entire scene had been intentionally staged. An unidentified fingerprint was found in the blood on the steering wheel, but police were never able to match it to Mary or any known suspect. Mary's purse, her car keys, and all of her outer clothing were missing.

The initial investigation was stumped. Police were puzzled as to how an abduction, one that apparently involved forcing a woman to strip, could have occurred in a busy, well-lit car park without a single witness. The theory that she had been taken elsewhere and the car returned seemed more plausible, but it raised its own set of confusing questions. Why would an attacker risk being caught by returning the car to the scene, and why would they leave such a strange tableau of evidence behind?

Investigators turned to Mary's personal life and discovered it was more complicated than her happy, newlywed status suggested. She had recently received roses from an unknown "secret admirer" and had been bothered by "worrying" phone calls. Co-workers had overheard parts of these calls. On one occasion, she was heard saying, "I'm a married woman now." In another, even more cryptic exchange, she told the caller, "You can come over to my house anytime you like, I can't come over there." This statement suggested to some that she was not having an affair, as she would likely be sneaking to the other person's location; rather, it hinted that she was afraid of the caller and wanted any meeting to be on her own territory, perhaps when her husband was present. This fear was reinforced by a conversation she had with a friend weeks earlier, in which she admitted she was worried about being home alone and, specifically, being in her car alone.

Her husband, Roy Little, was briefly scrutinized. He had a rock-solid alibi, as he was sixty miles (about ninety-six kilometers) away and seen by numerous people at his work training. Police never considered him a suspect. His behavior, however, was noted by many as strange. He appeared publicly unemotional, expressed more concern about getting his car back than about the search for his wife, and refused to take multiple lie detector tests. While suspicious to a modern eye, some context has been offered regarding the cultural expectations of male stoicism in the 1960s.

For a month, the case was a complete dead end. Then, the investigation was thrown wide open when evidence emerged that Mary had been taken across state lines, making it a federal offense and bringing in the FBI. Mary's credit card had been used. The first charge was made in the early morning hours of October 15, around 2:00 a.m., at a gas station in Charlotte, North Carolina. The second charge appeared later that same day, around midday, at another gas station in Raleigh, North Carolina.

Detectives raced to North Carolina and retrieved the receipts. The signature on the slip from Charlotte read "Mrs. Roy H. Little Jr." and was confidently identified as Mary's handwriting. The gas station attendants from both locations were interviewed and clearly remembered the encounters. The attendant in Charlotte recalled a woman with a bleeding cut on her head, who was trying to hide her face while a man with her "barked orders" at her. The attendant in Raleigh described an even more grim scene: the woman was covered in blood, including blood running down her legs, and she was in the company of two men, both of whom were ordering her around.

This new information created an impossible, contradictory timeline. At the exact same time Mary was reportedly being seen with two men in Raleigh — midday on October 15 — her car was being discovered by her boss back in the Atlanta car park. This implied a highly complex crime involving at least three individuals: the two men with Mary in North Carolina, and a third accomplice who drove her car forty-one unaccounted-for miles (about sixty-five kilometers) before returning it to the Lenox Square lot.

The choice of location was just as baffling. Charlotte, North Carolina, was Mary's hometown, the place where her parents still lived. Taking an abductee to the one place she was most likely to be recognized was an audacious risk. It suggested the attackers were either astonishingly reckless or, perhaps, knew exactly where she was from and were taunting her. This link to Charlotte was strengthened by another clue: a license plate, stolen from Charlotte, was reportedly found on the car the group was using in North Carolina. The psychological profile of the lead attacker was terrifying: a man who took bizarre risks, was clever, and was utterly unafraid of being caught.

In the years that followed, the case grew colder but stranger. In 1966, an inmate in a Georgia prison told the FBI that two men had confessed to him that they were paid $5,000 to kidnap Mary. They claimed they took her to a small greenhouse in Mount Holly, killed her, and buried her there. Investigators located a property that matched the description, but it had recently been demolished, leaving them with another dead end.

Then, in May 1967, the case took another sinister turn. A woman named Diane Shields, the secretary who had been hired to take over Mary's job at the C&S Bank, was found murdered. Her body was discovered in the trunk of her car; she had been suffocated with a scarf and paper shoved down her throat. She was fully clothed, and her diamond engagement ring was still on her finger, ruling out sexual assault and robbery as motives. The case remains unsolved, but police have long speculated it was linked to Mary's disappearance.

This potential link fueled theories that the disappearances were connected to a scandal at the bank. Around the time Mary went missing, the bank had a former FBI agent investigating rumors of a small prostitution ring and "lesbian sexual assaults" among the staff. Mary's boss insisted she knew nothing about it, but other sources claimed she did. The fact that both Mary and her replacement were murdered suggested they may have known something that made them a threat. In a final, inexplicable twist, after a detective publicly suggested the two cases were linked, Mary's mother called him. A year and a half after her daughter had vanished, she told the detective to "leave it" and that she did not want Mary's case looked into anymore.

Other potential leads, like a $20,000 ransom call that was deemed a hoax and a report of another woman being lured in the same car park just ten minutes before Mary's disappearance, all led nowhere. A full review of the case in 2009, using modern forensic technology, made no progress. The files related to Mary Shotwell Little's disappearance have reportedly since been lost. The staged car, the cryptic phone calls, the contradictory timeline, and the chilling North Carolina sightings have hardened into one of Atlanta's most enduring and perplexing unsolved mysteries.

CONCLUSION

As you close this book, you are left with a chilling realization: evil rarely announces itself with a roar. More often, it moves in silence, hiding behind a neighbor's door or beneath the mask of an ordinary life. Through these twenty-four stories, I have traced the darkest outlines of the human experience — from the scams that exploited blind ambition to the cults that devoured the will, and the crimes that time very nearly managed to erase.

Finishing these chapters does not mean the danger has passed. The cases presented here serve as stark reminders that justice is often a winding path, and truth is frequently more terrifying than any urban legend. These accounts force us to ask an uncomfortable question: how many more secrets remain buried in forgotten files, waiting for the light of day?

I hope this journey into the unknown has prompted you to look at the world through a different lens. The next time you hear an unexplained creak in the floorboards, spot an unfamiliar van idling in your neighborhood, or read a headline that seems too strange to be true, remember that behind every anomaly lies a story just as cold as the ones you've just finished.

Thank you for walking beside me through the shadows. Keep the lights on, stay vigilant, and above all, never assume you truly know those around you. The world is far more complex — and much darker — than most of us dare to admit.

A SPECIAL THANK YOU FOR YOUR SUPPORT!

Thank you so much for purchasing this book and joining me on this journey into the shadows. As a token of my appreciation, I'd love to send you a special bonus — the digital versions of two of my best-selling books, completely free:

- 1,144 Random, Interesting & Fun Facts You Need to Know – The Knowledge Encyclopedia to Win Trivia
- Why Do We Say That? 101 Idioms, Phrases, Sayings & Facts! A Brief History on Where They Come From!

Scan the QR code below and enter your email, and I'll send the files directly to your inbox. Happy reading!

Thank You for Reading!

Thank you for joining me on this journey into the darkest corners of human nature. I hope this exploration of the mysteries behind these cases has challenged your theories and provided a clearer understanding of the search for justice.

If these haunting accounts have left an impression, I would be deeply grateful if you could leave a review on Amazon. Simply scan the QR code below to share your perspective. Reviews are the lifeblood of the true crime community, helping fellow armchair detectives and curious minds find the cases that deserve to be told.

Even a brief reflection makes a significant impact — and I truly appreciate your support in the pursuit of the truth.

See you in the next case file.

Scott